Life Is Strange

by David Hay

First published in 2014
by Sambolino Books

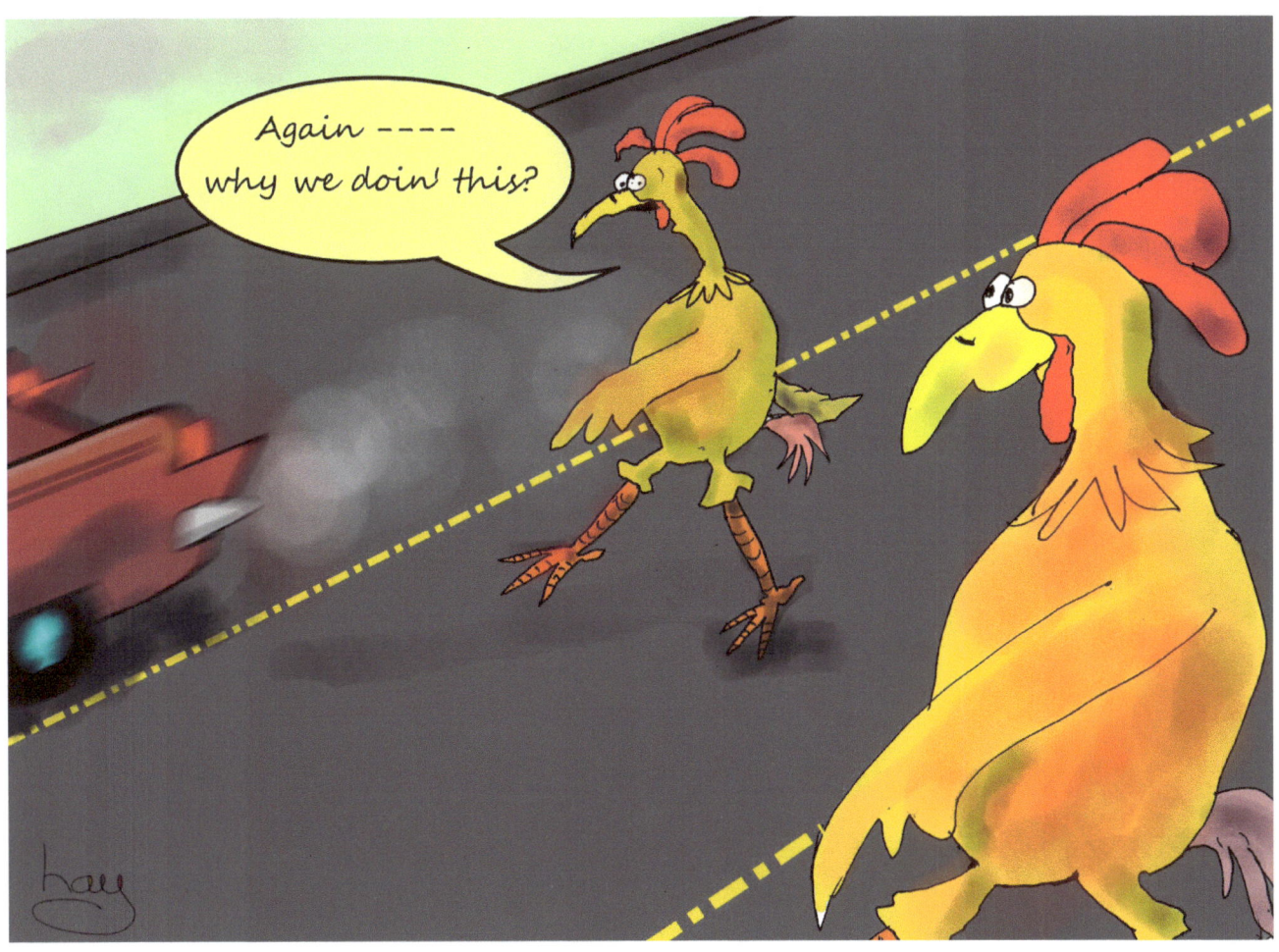

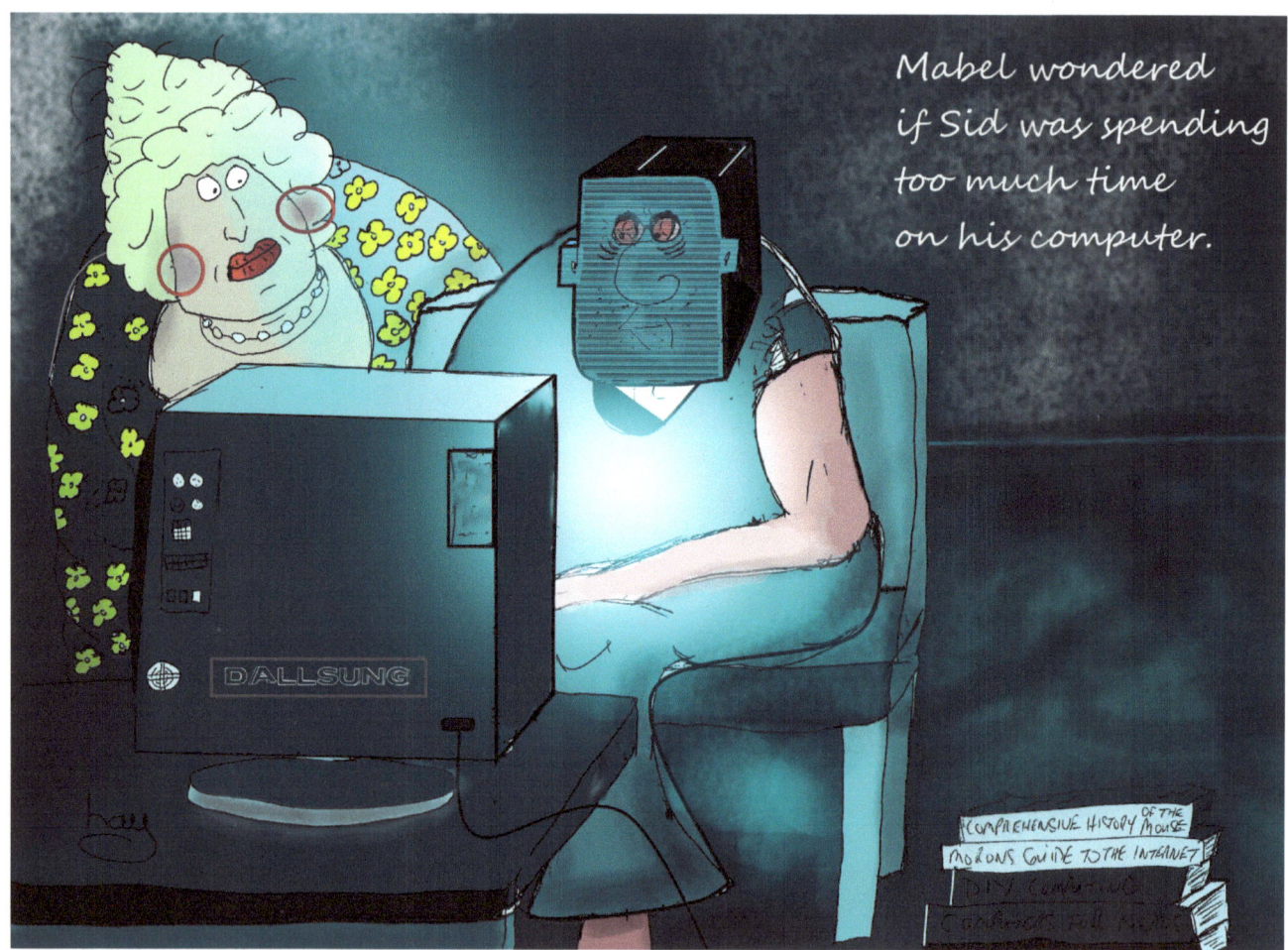

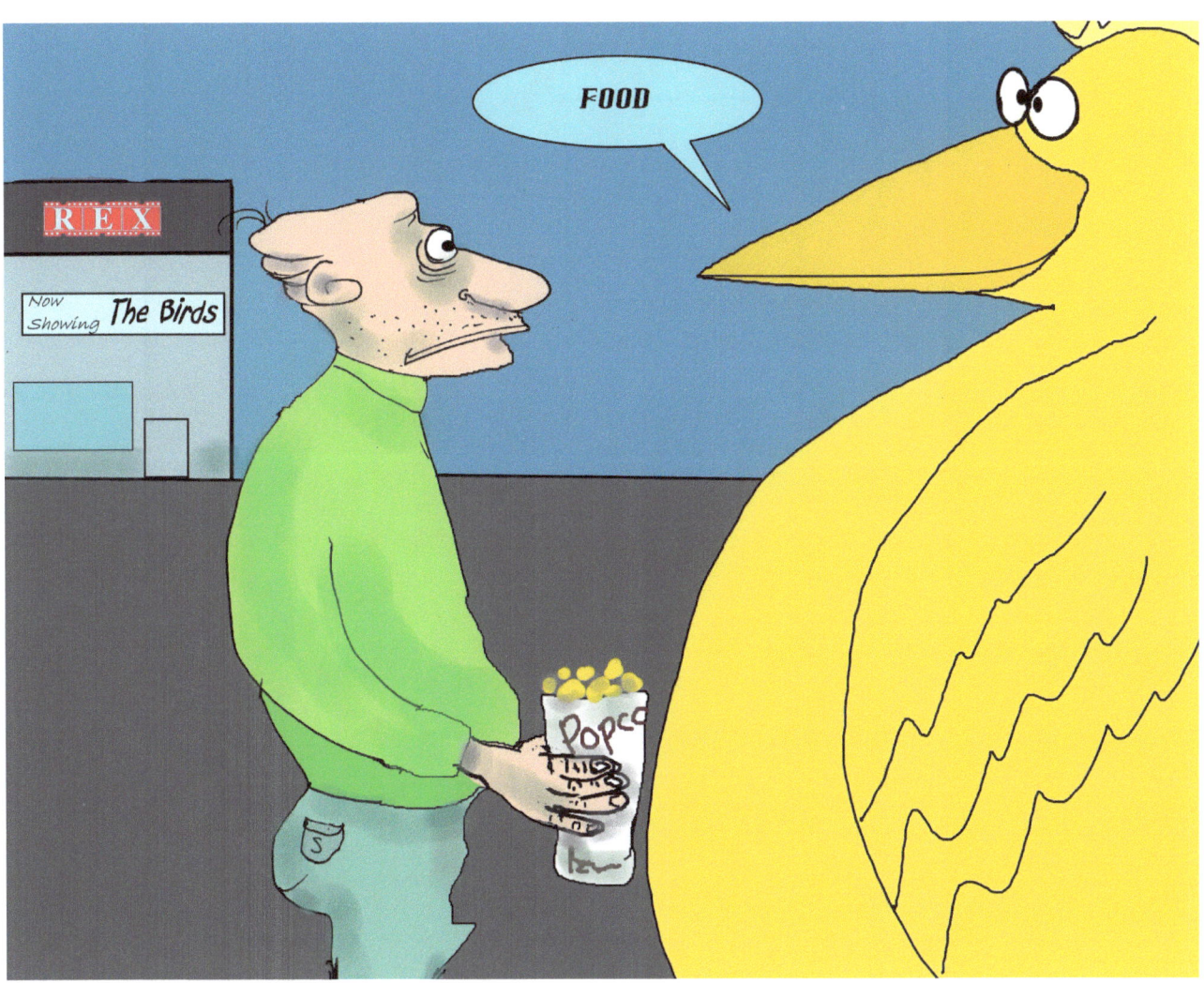

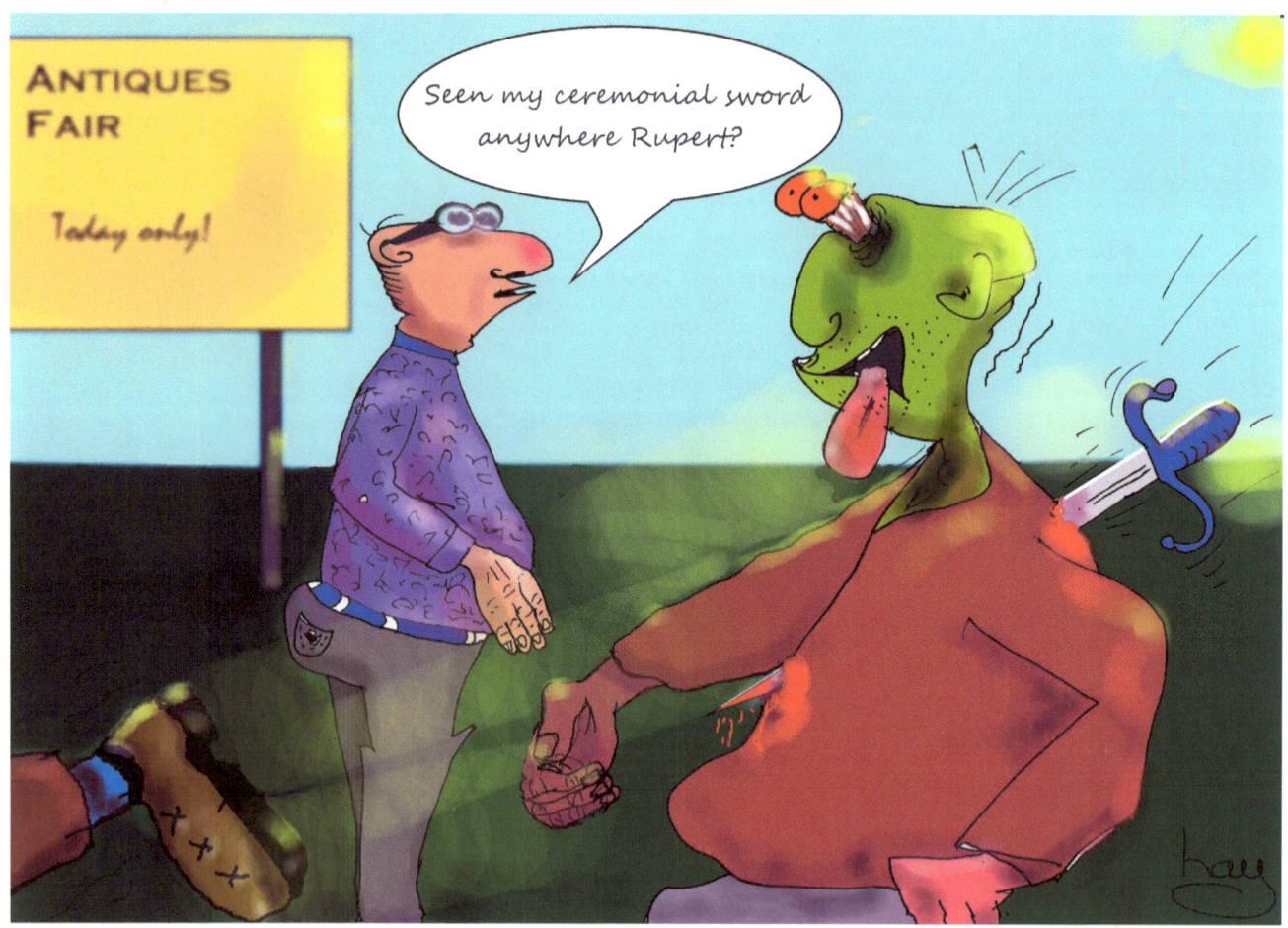

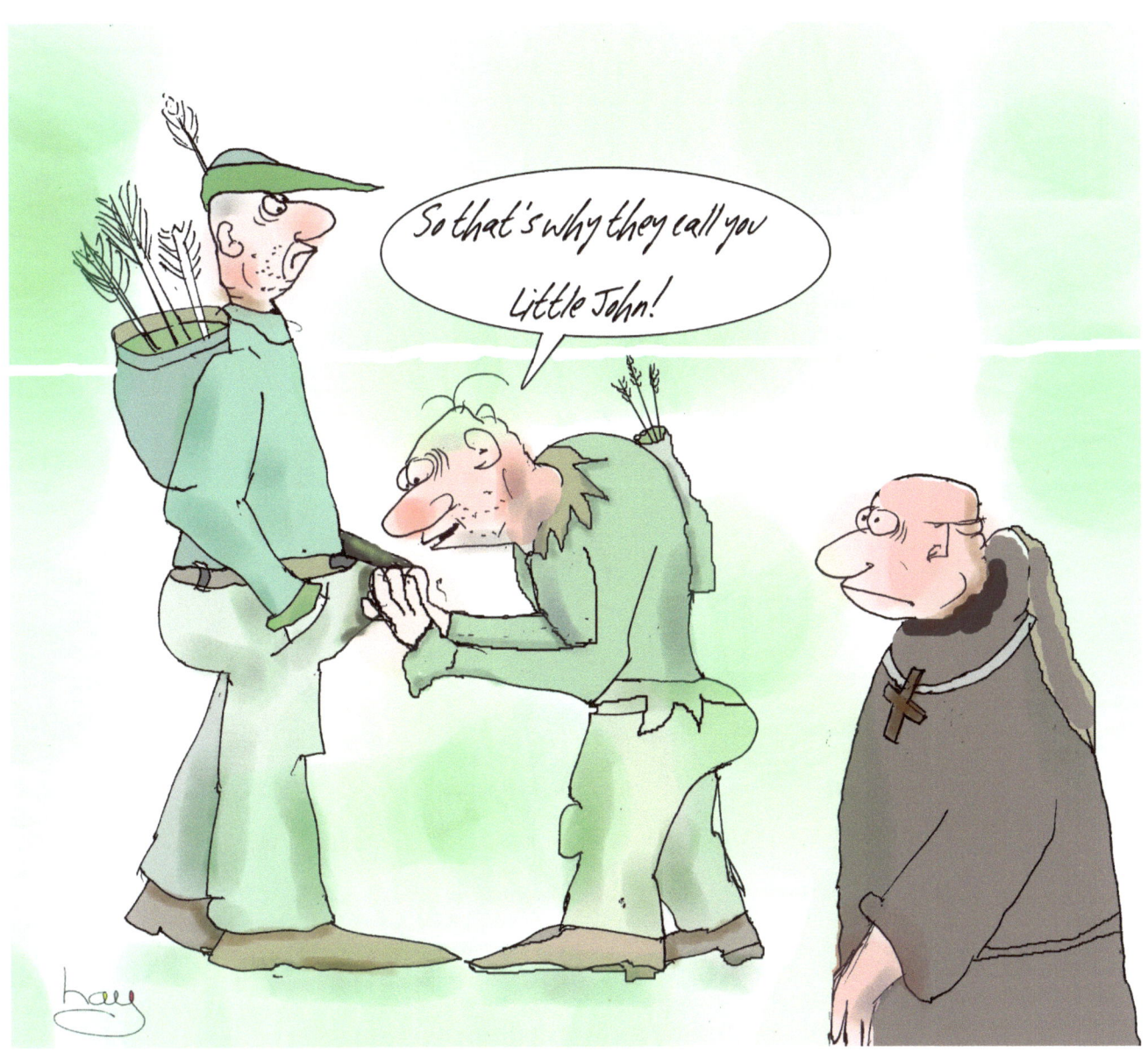

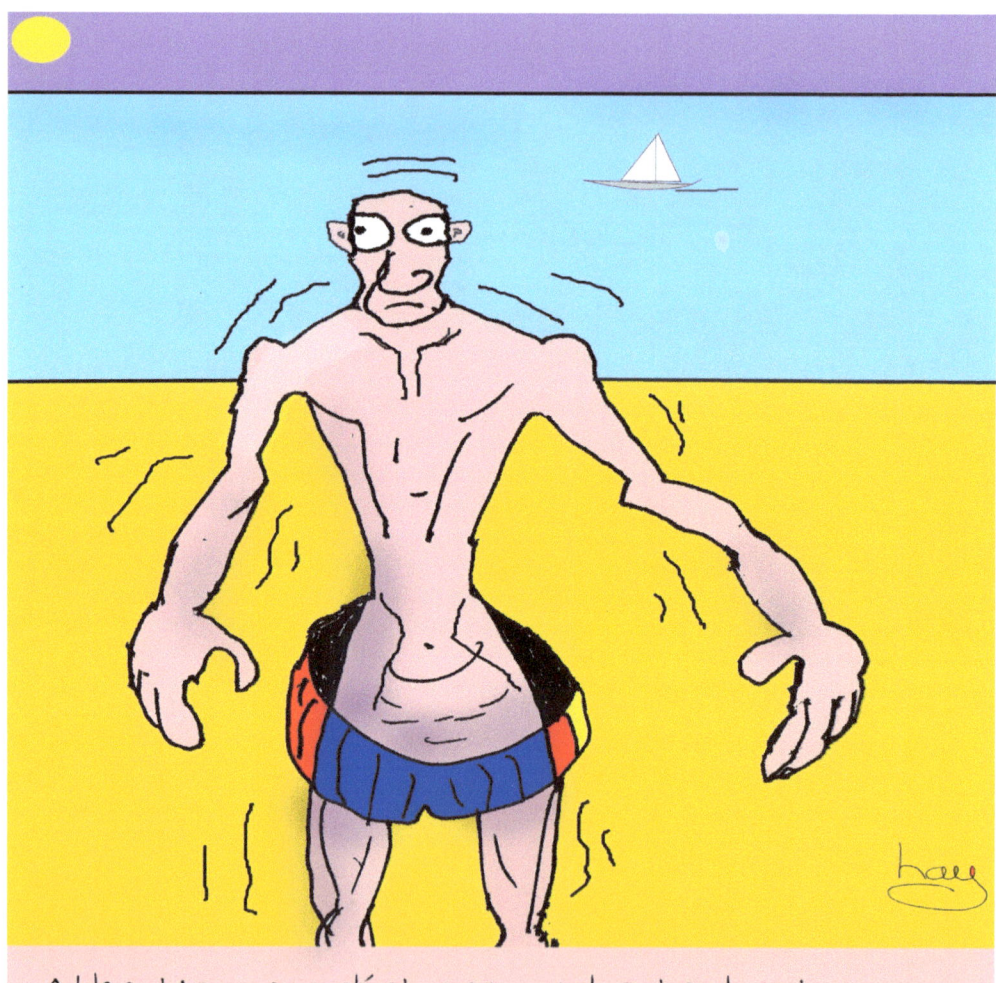

Albert's new diet seemed a tad extreme

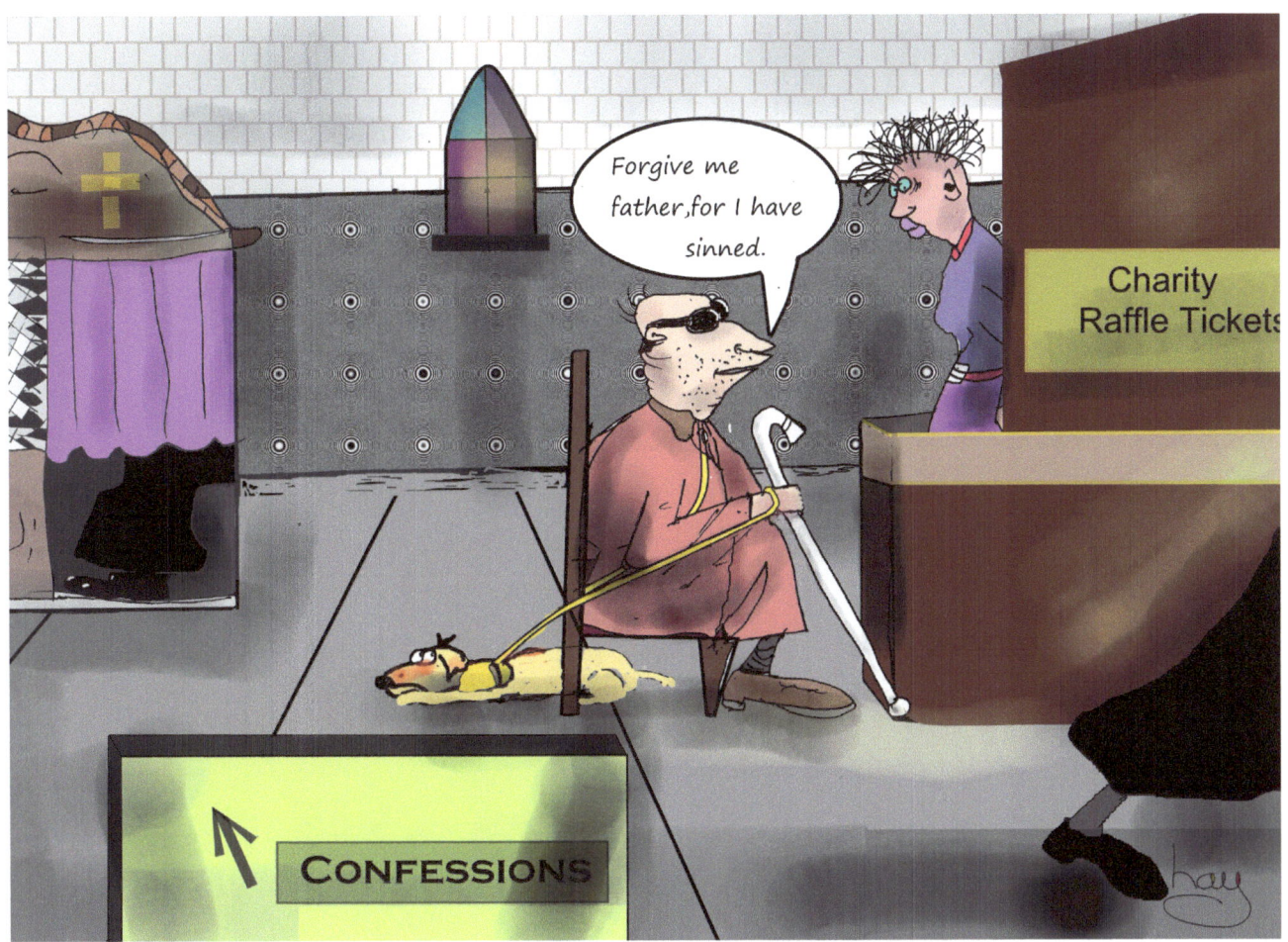

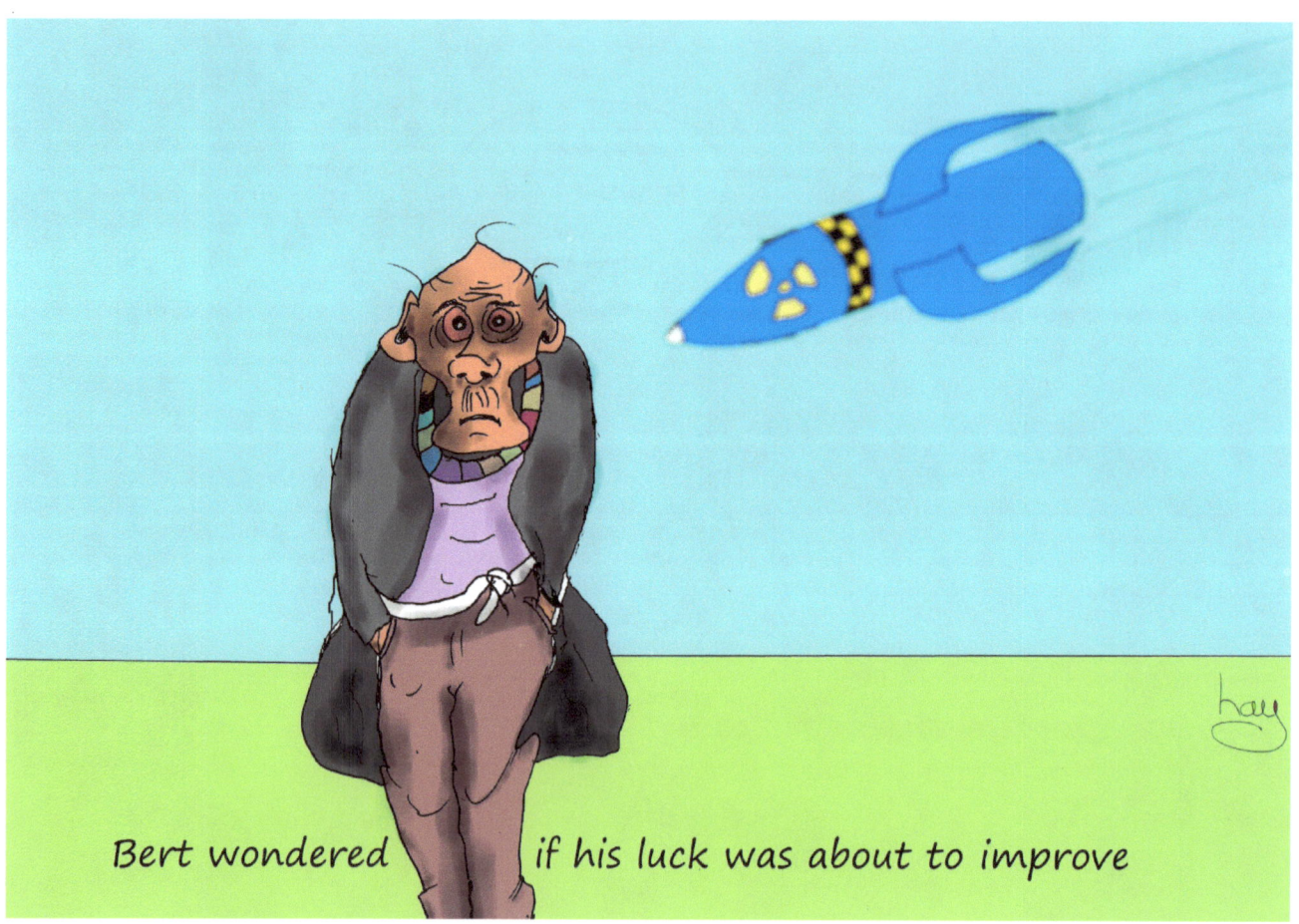

Bert wondered   if his luck was about to improve

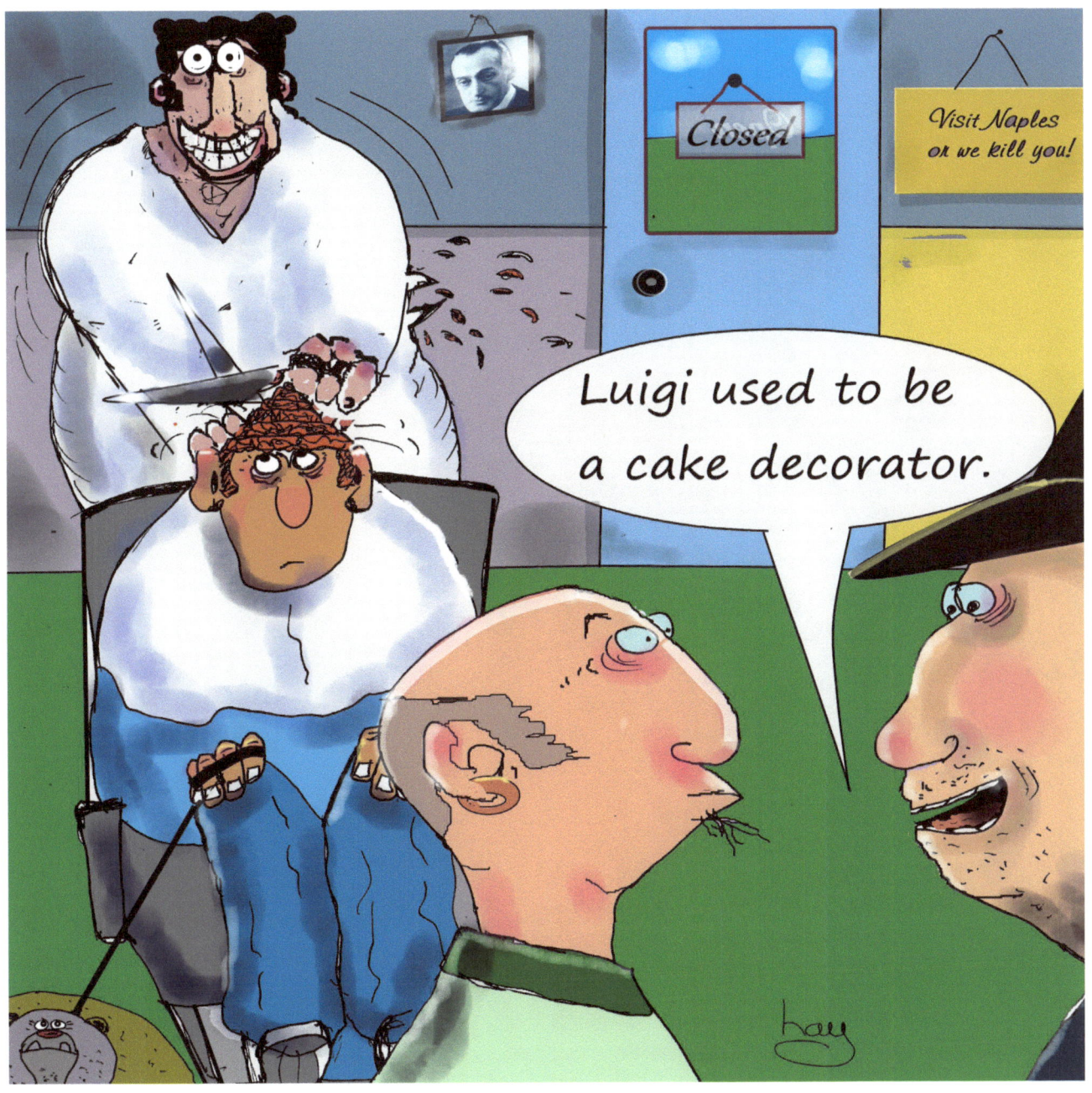

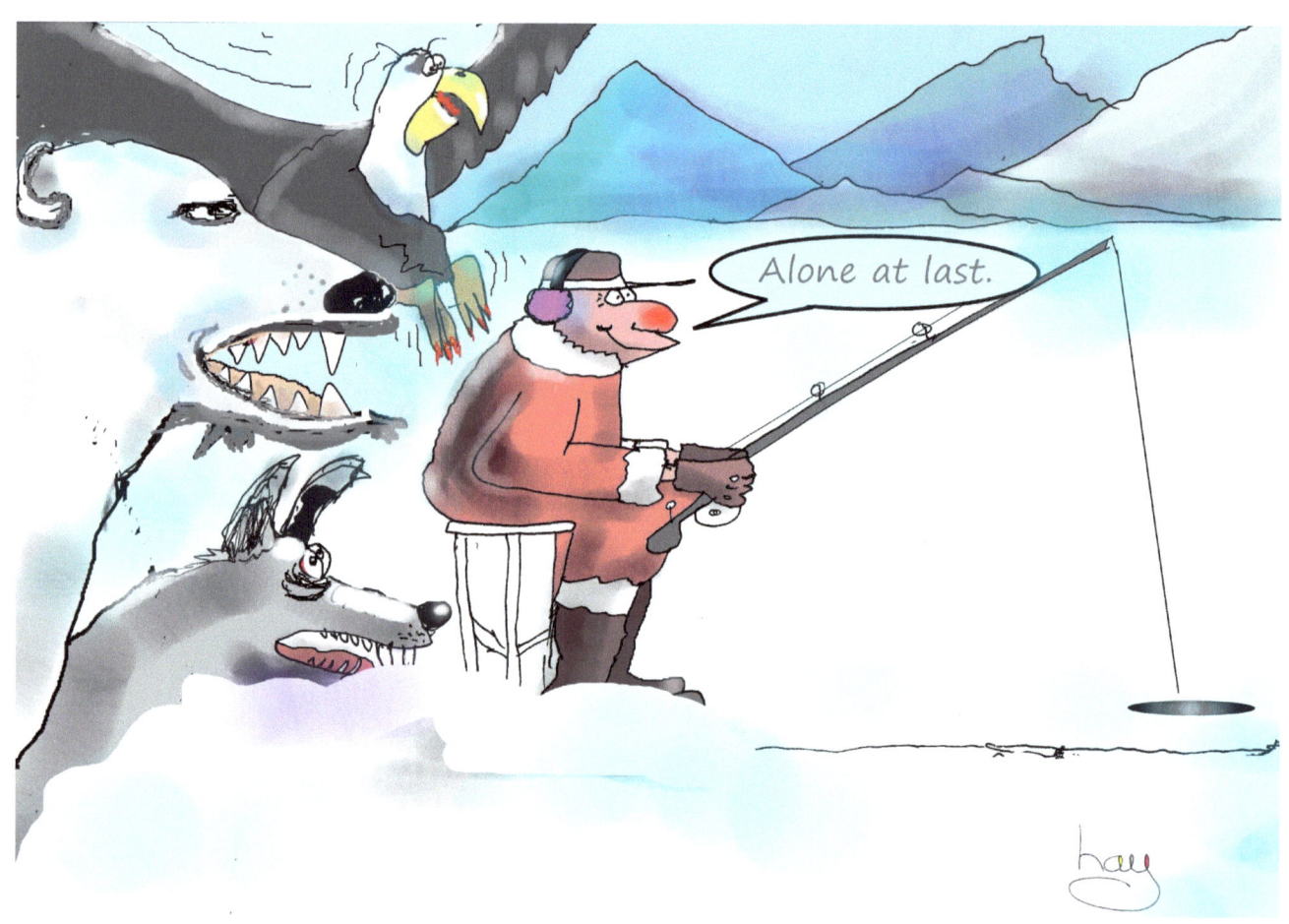

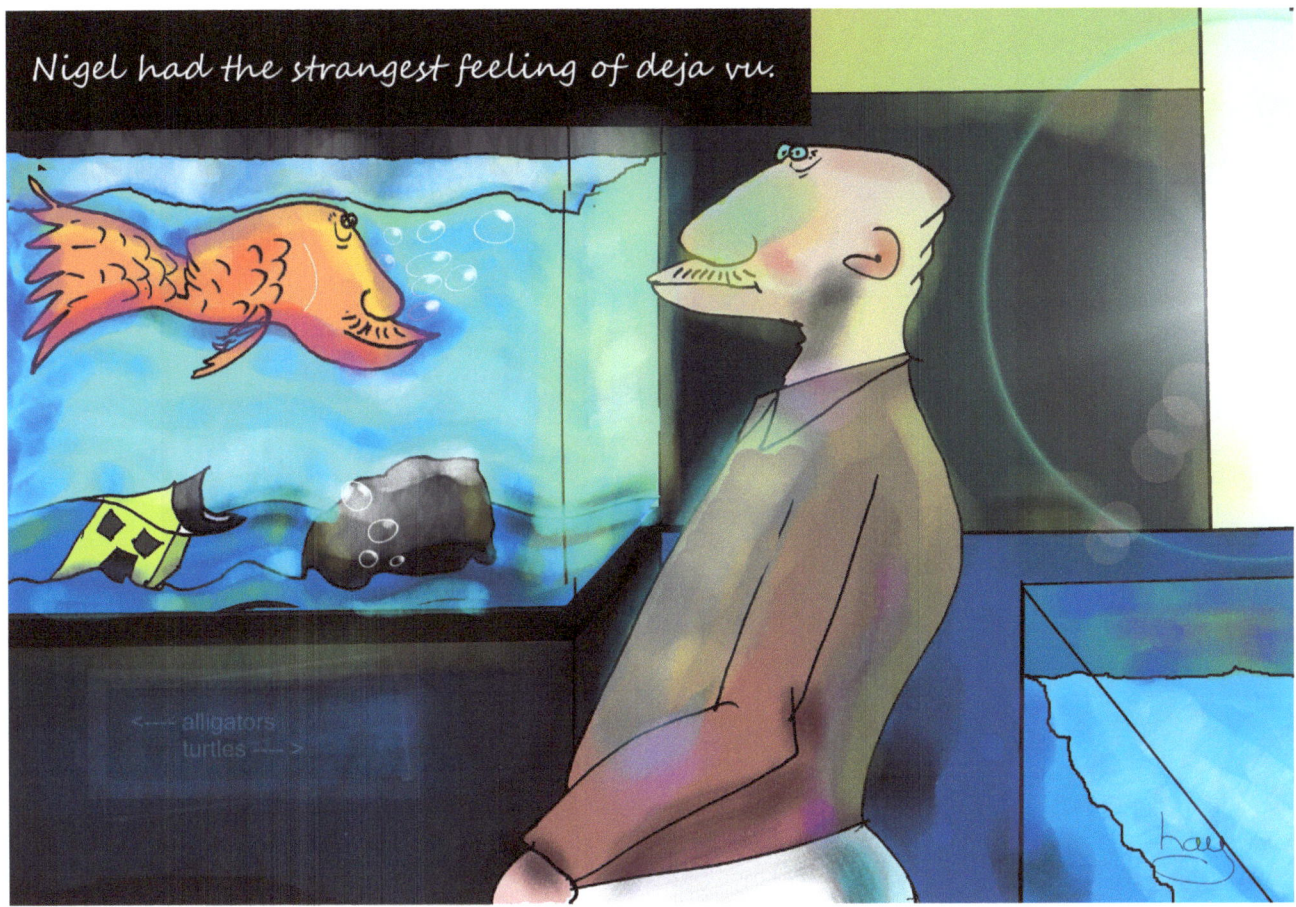

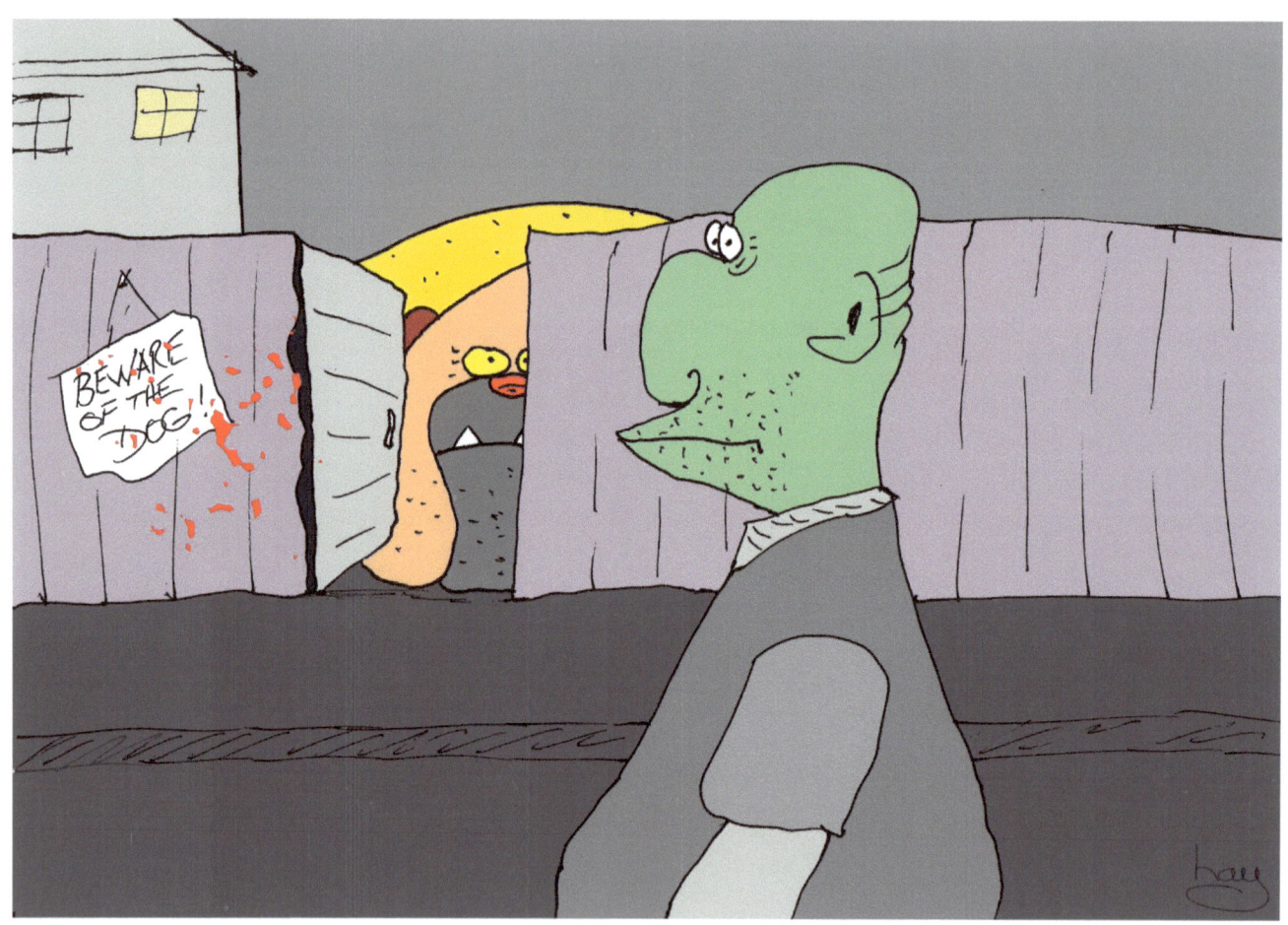

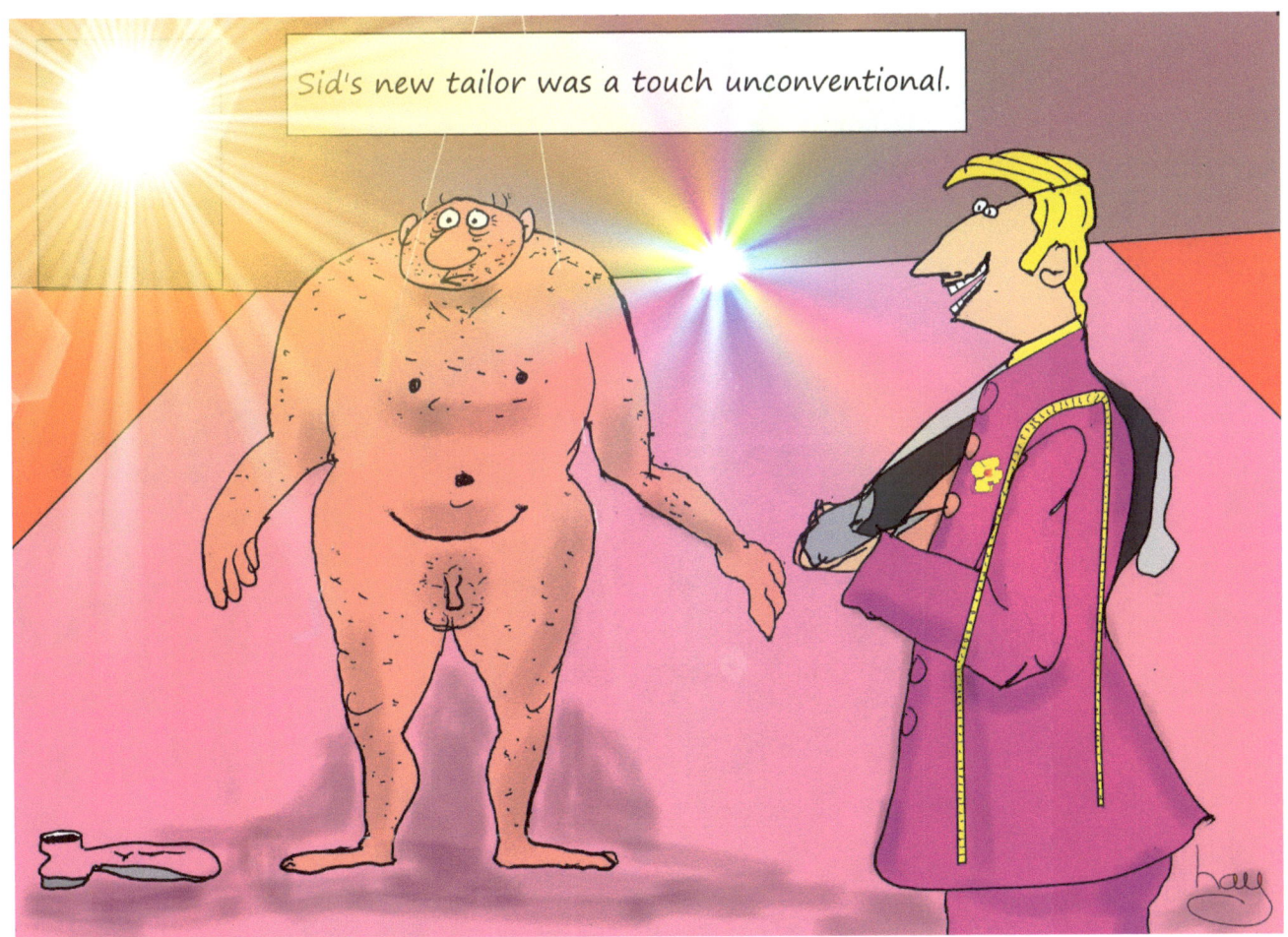

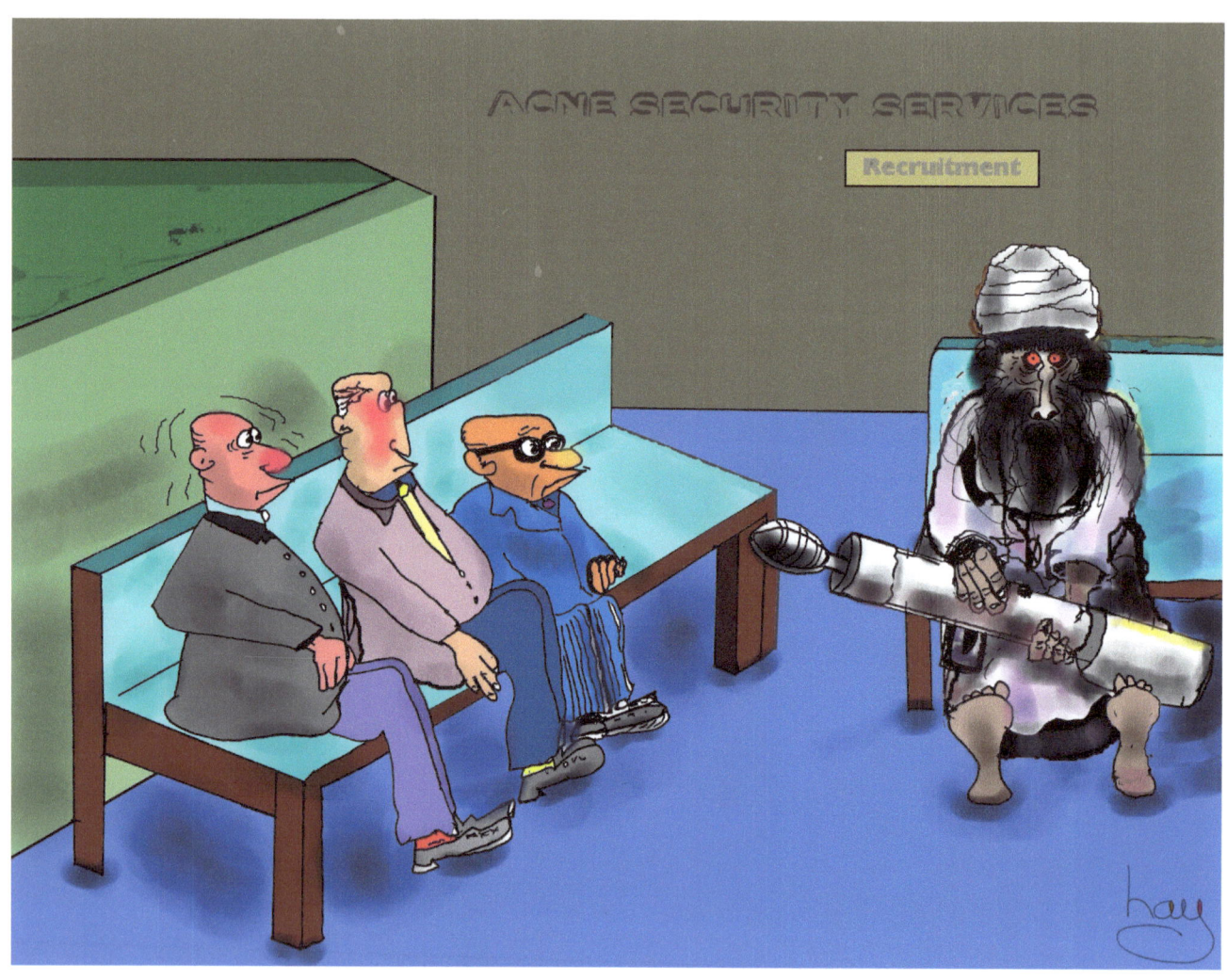

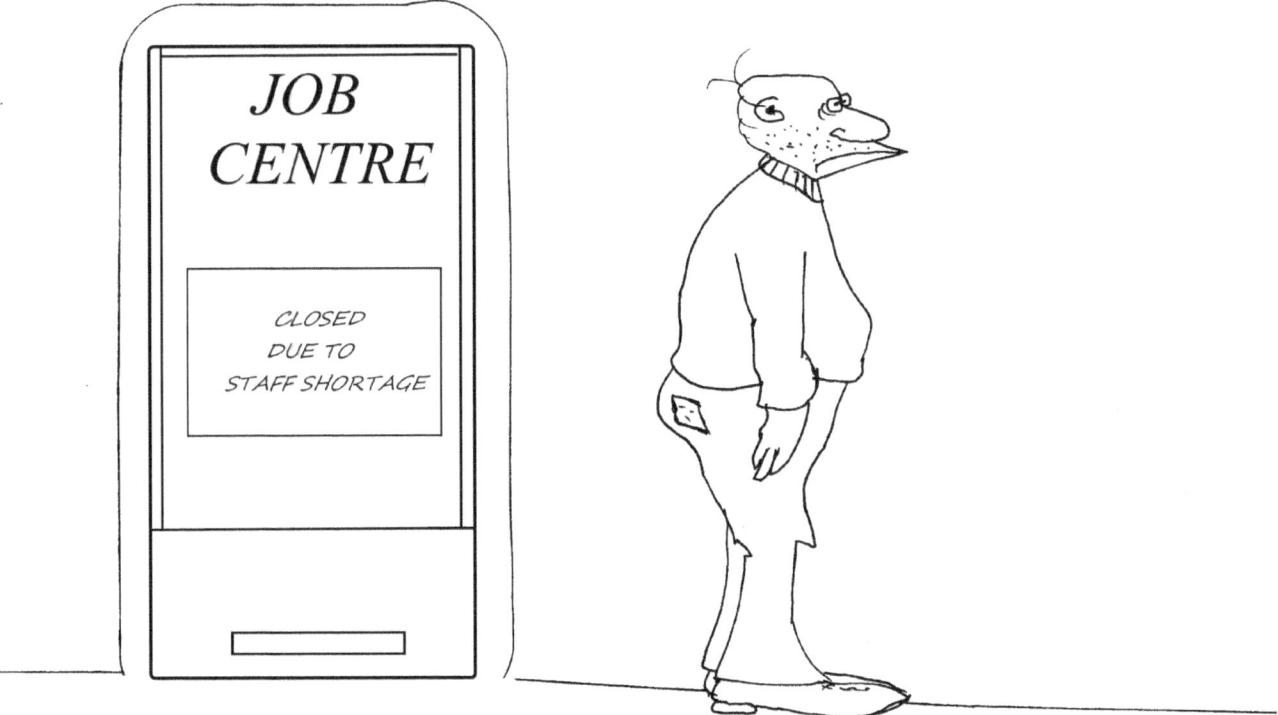

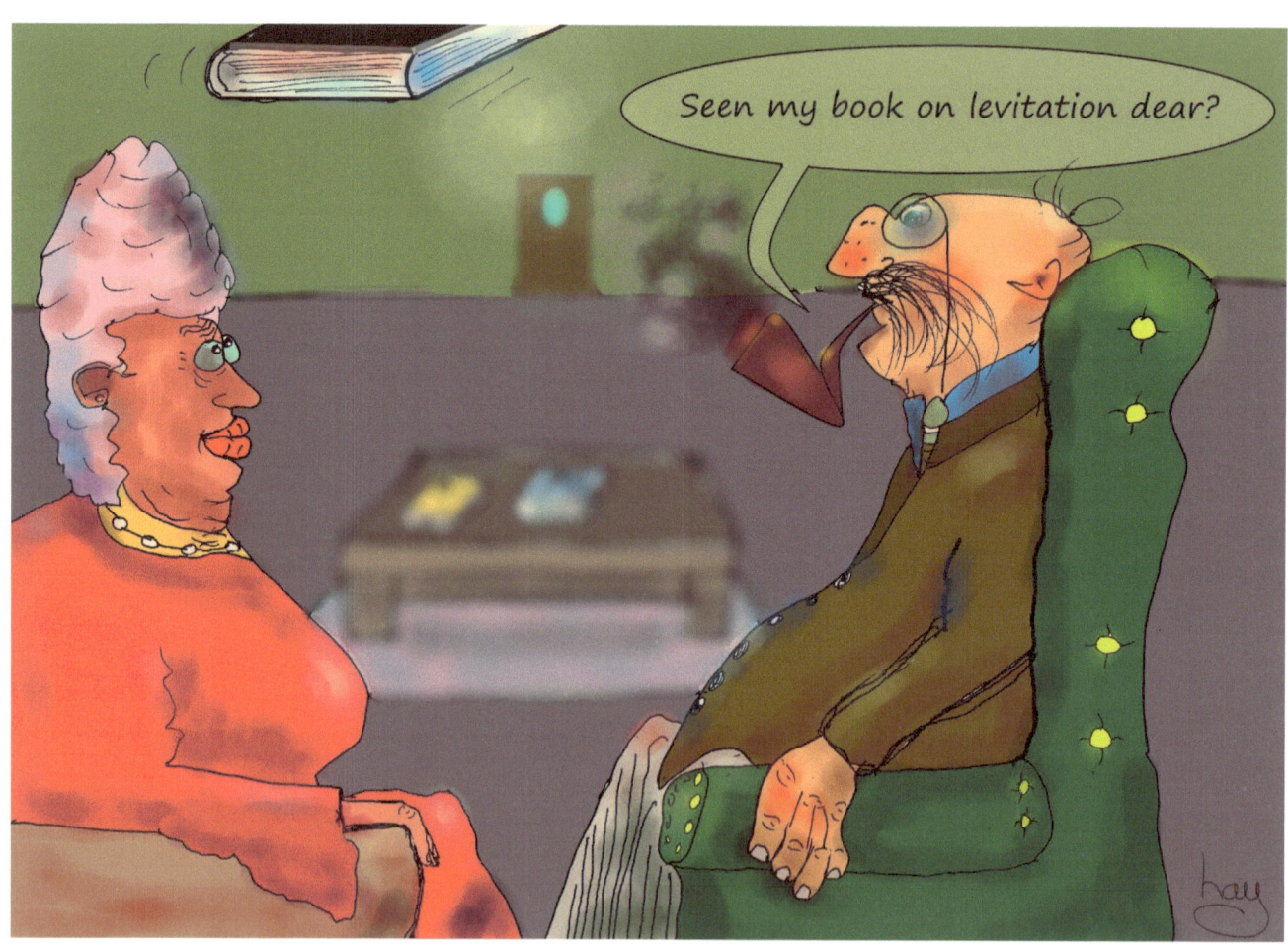

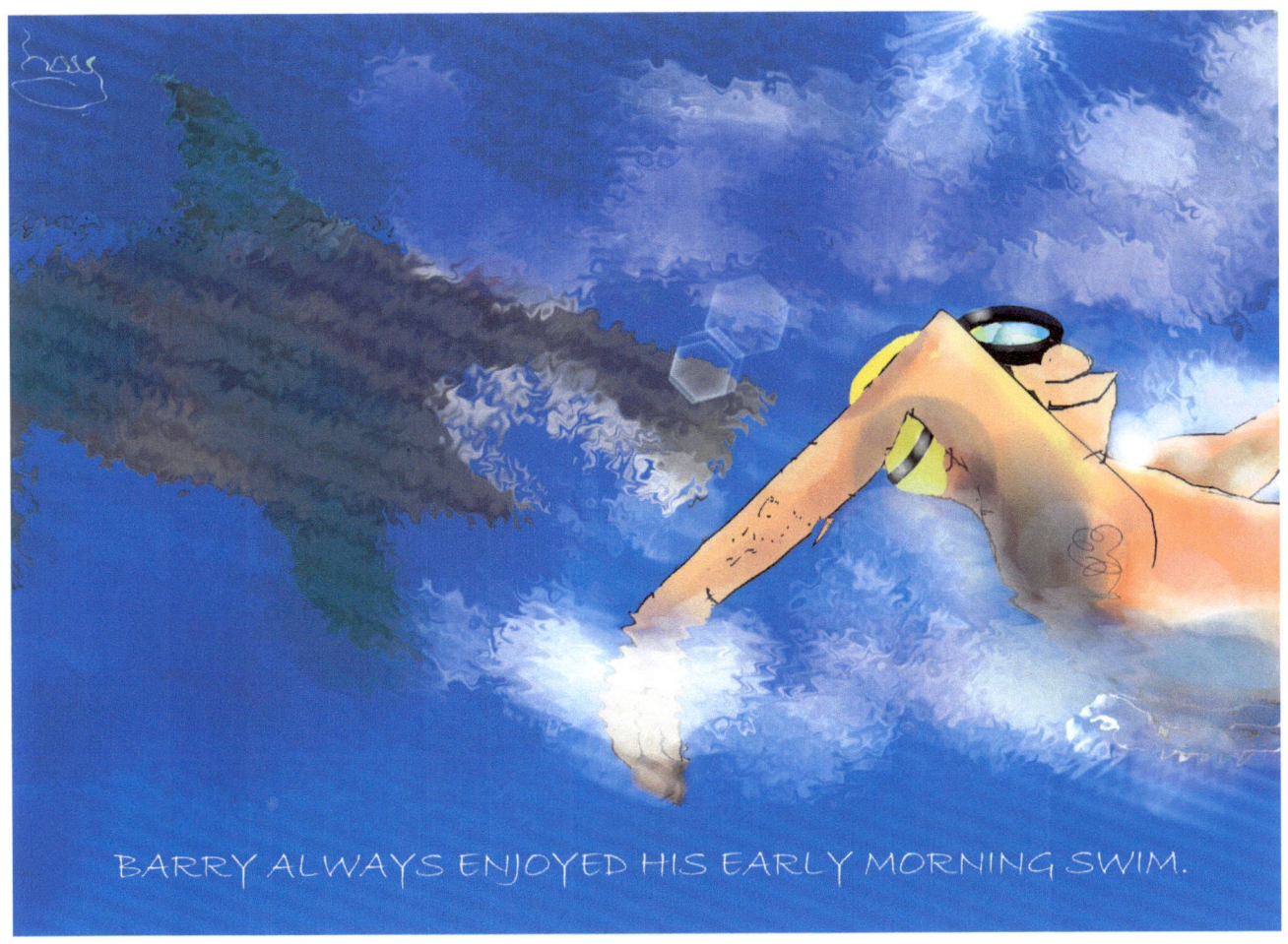

BARRY ALWAYS ENJOYED HIS EARLY MORNING SWIM.

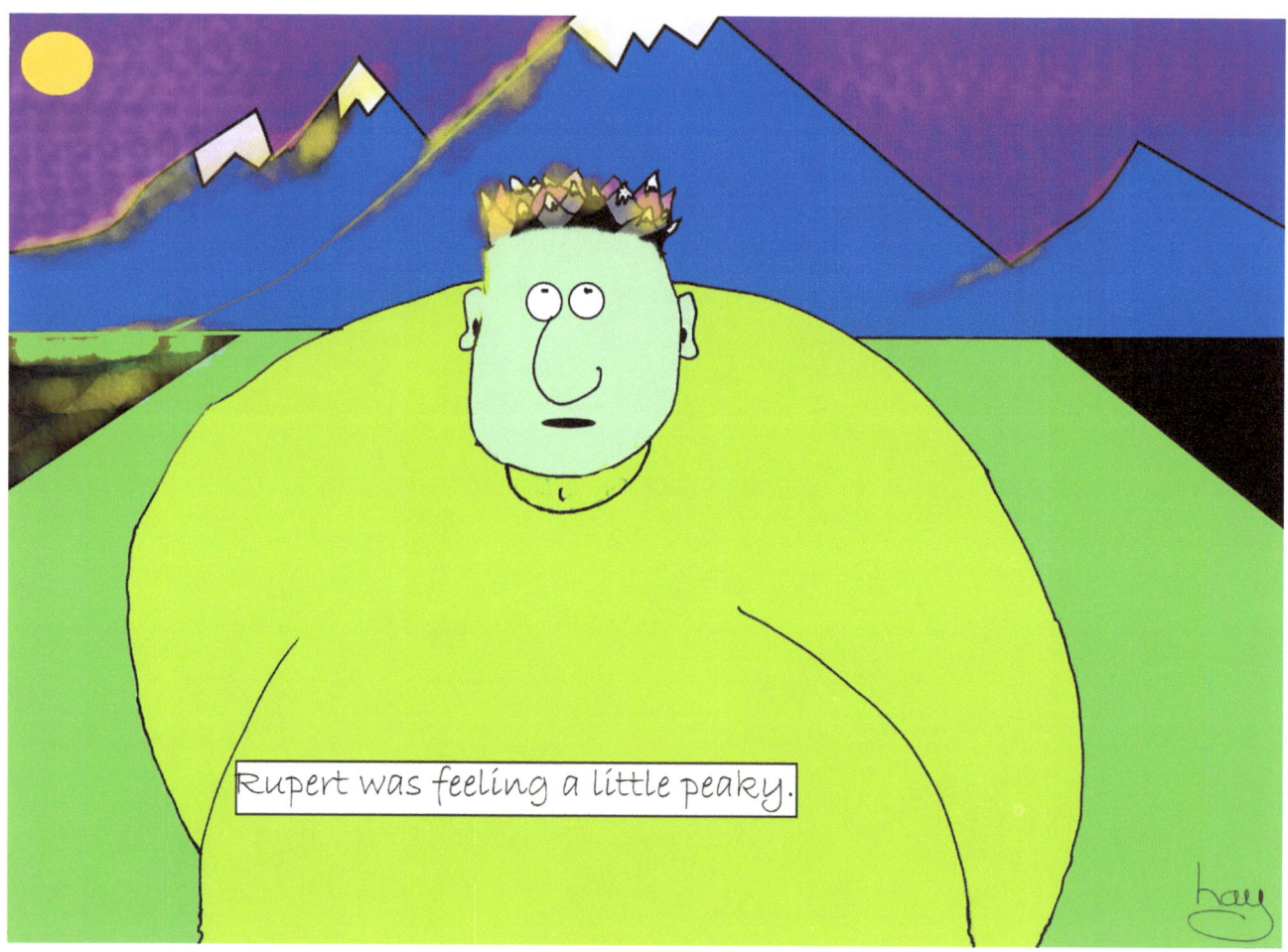

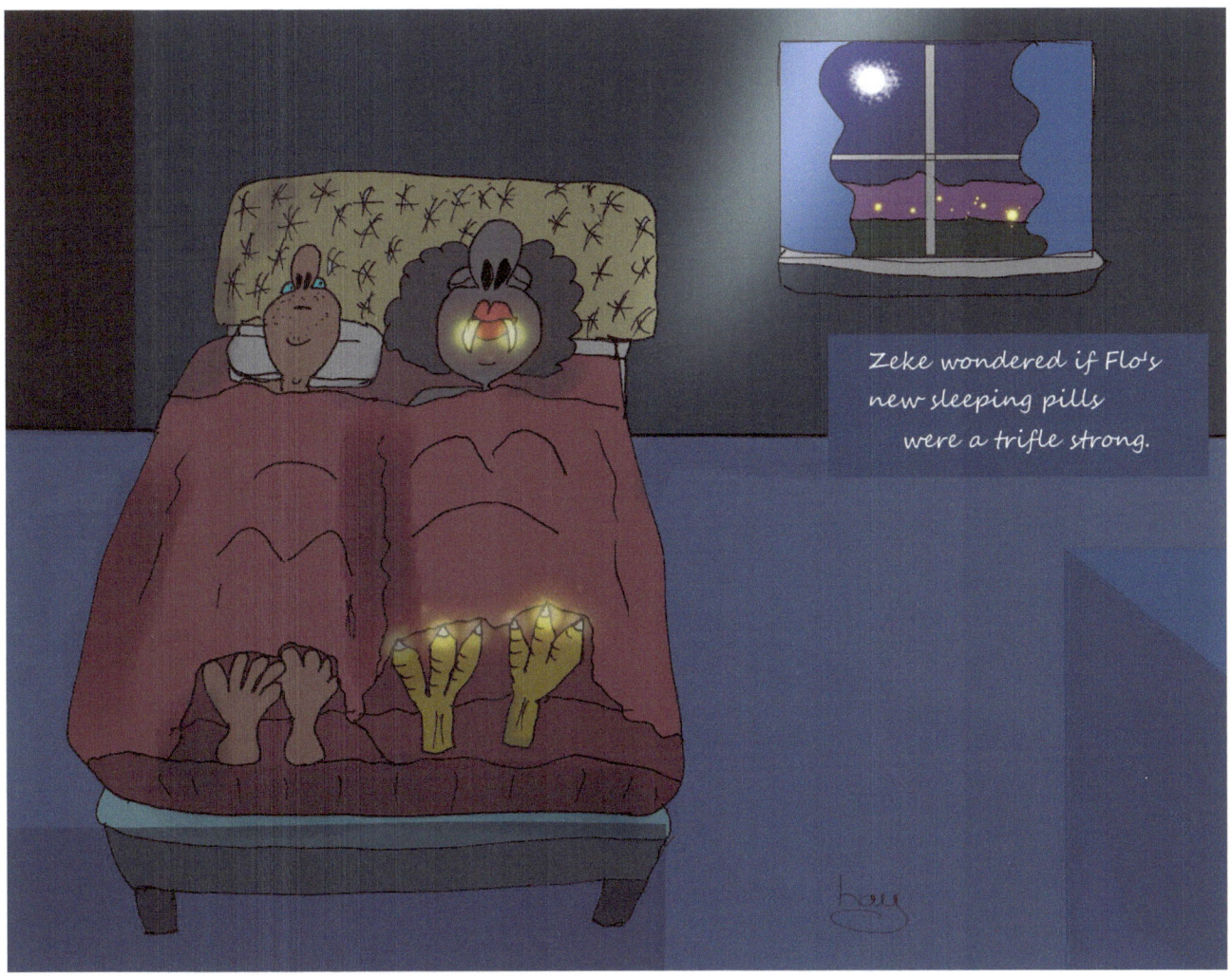

Zeke wondered if Flo's
new sleeping pills
were a trifle strong.

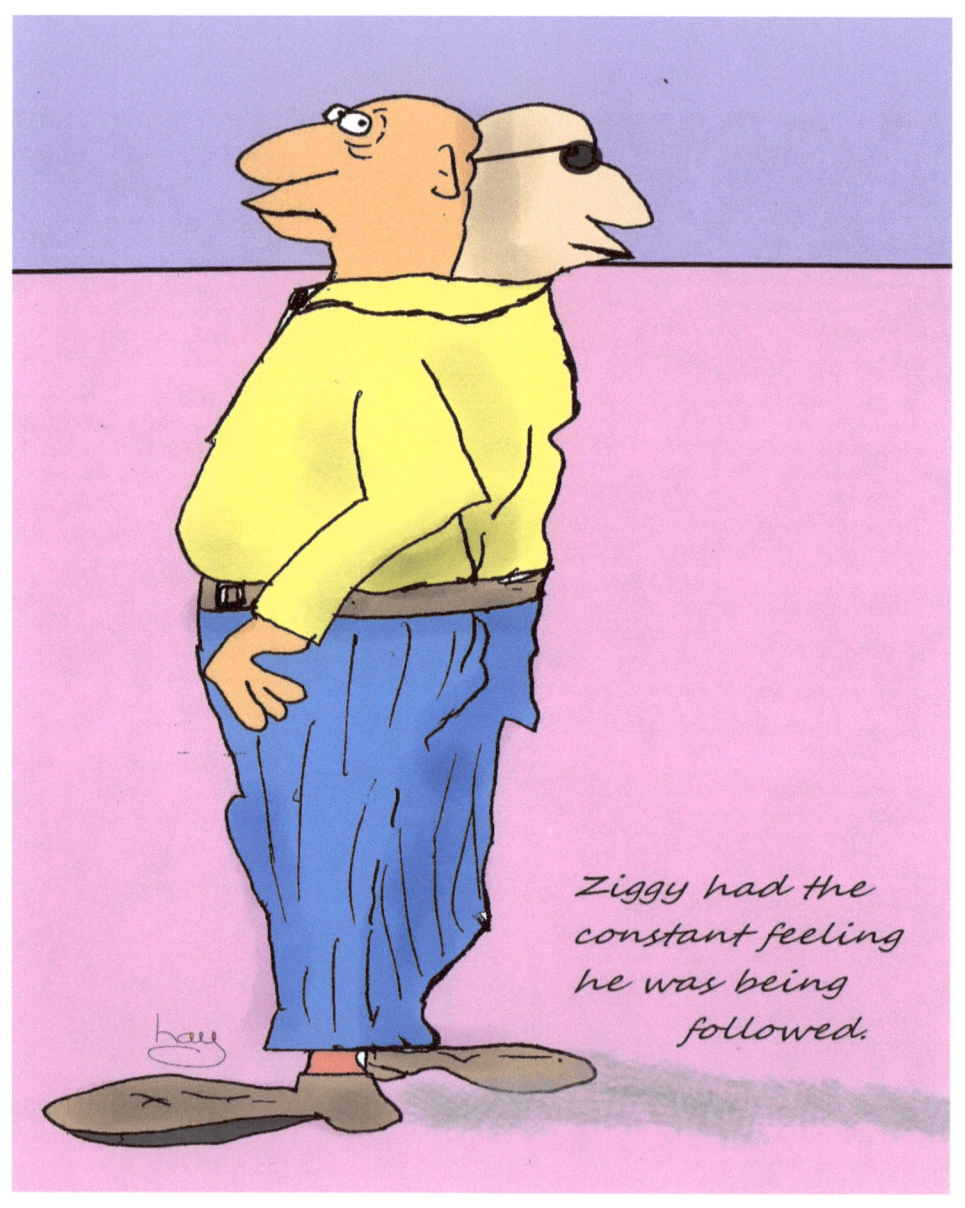

Ziggy had the
constant feeling
he was being
followed.

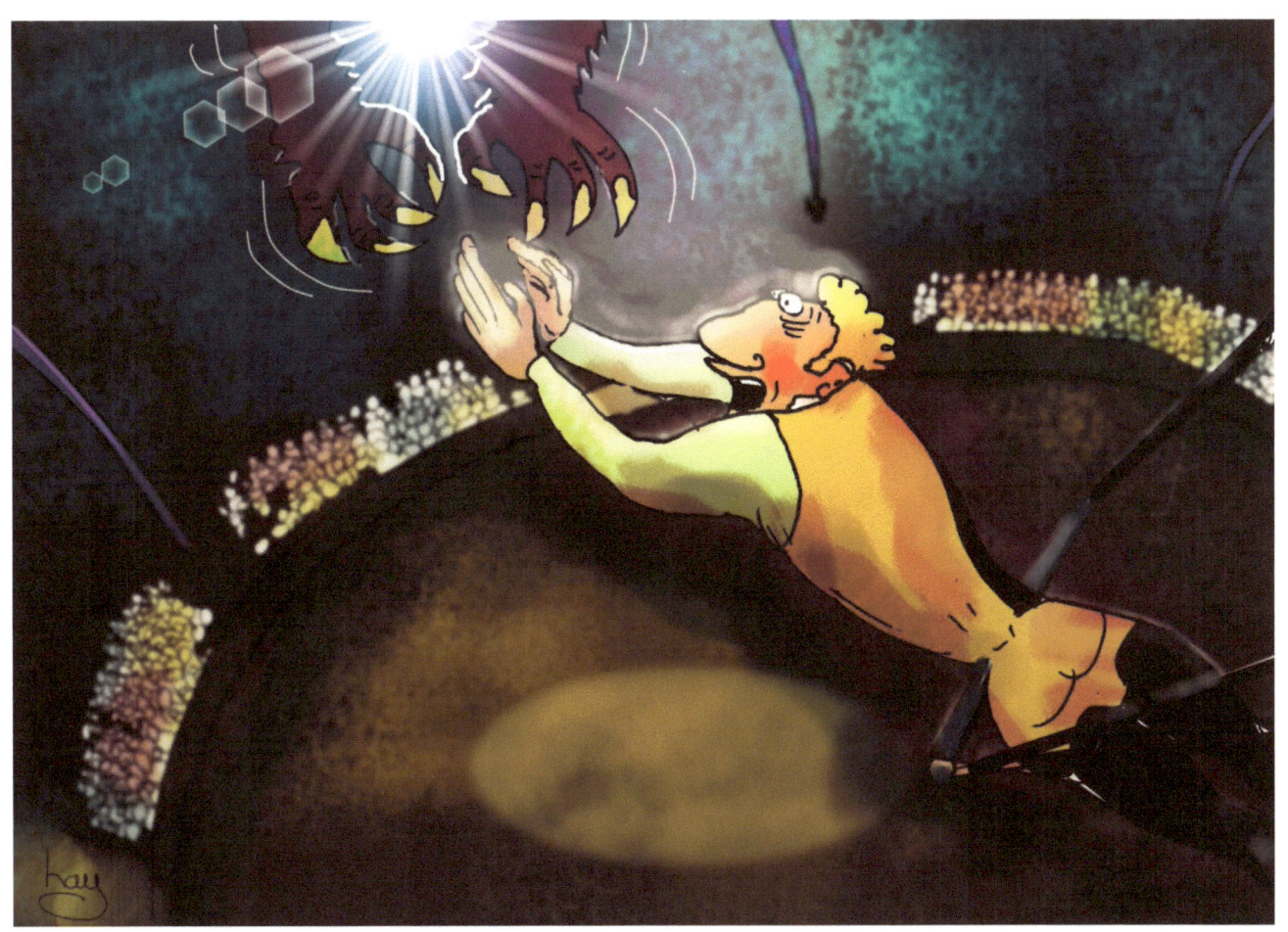

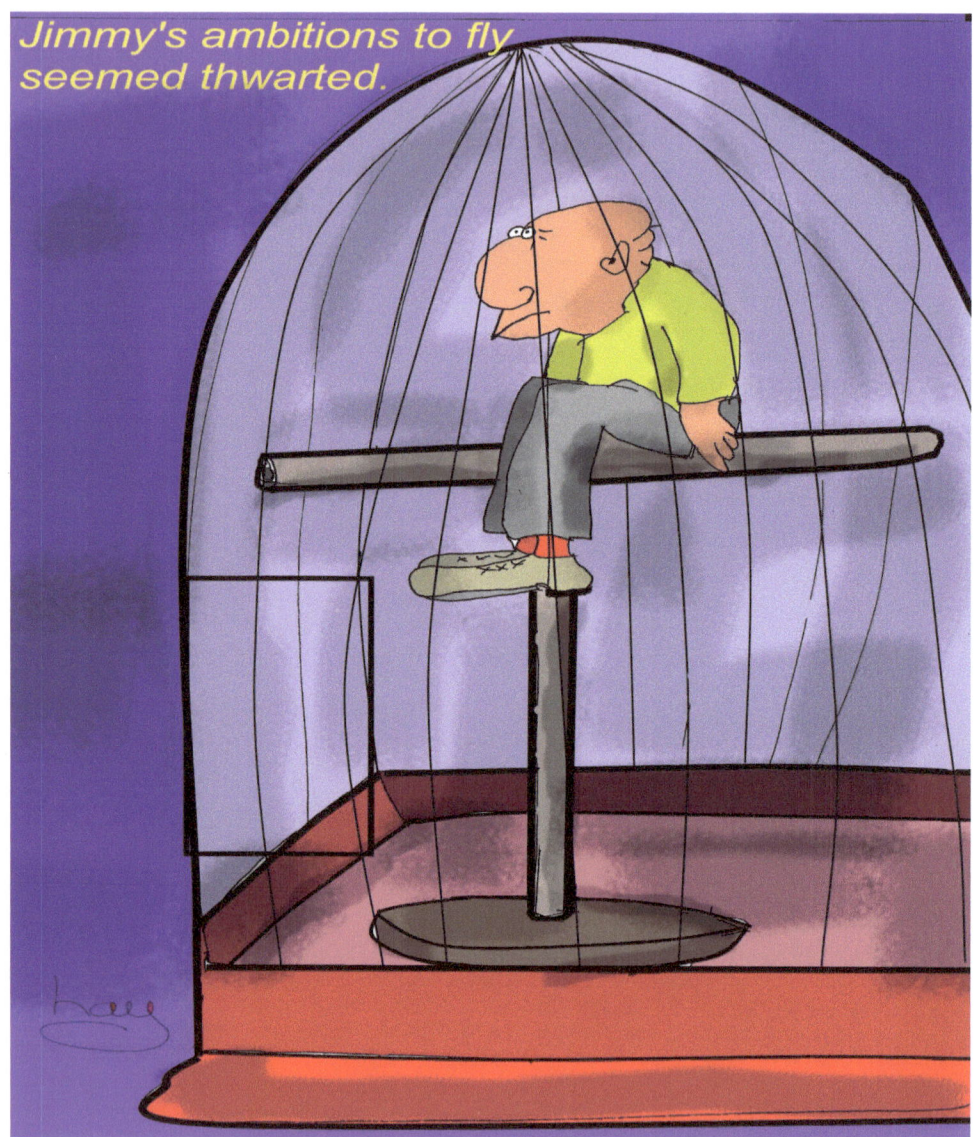

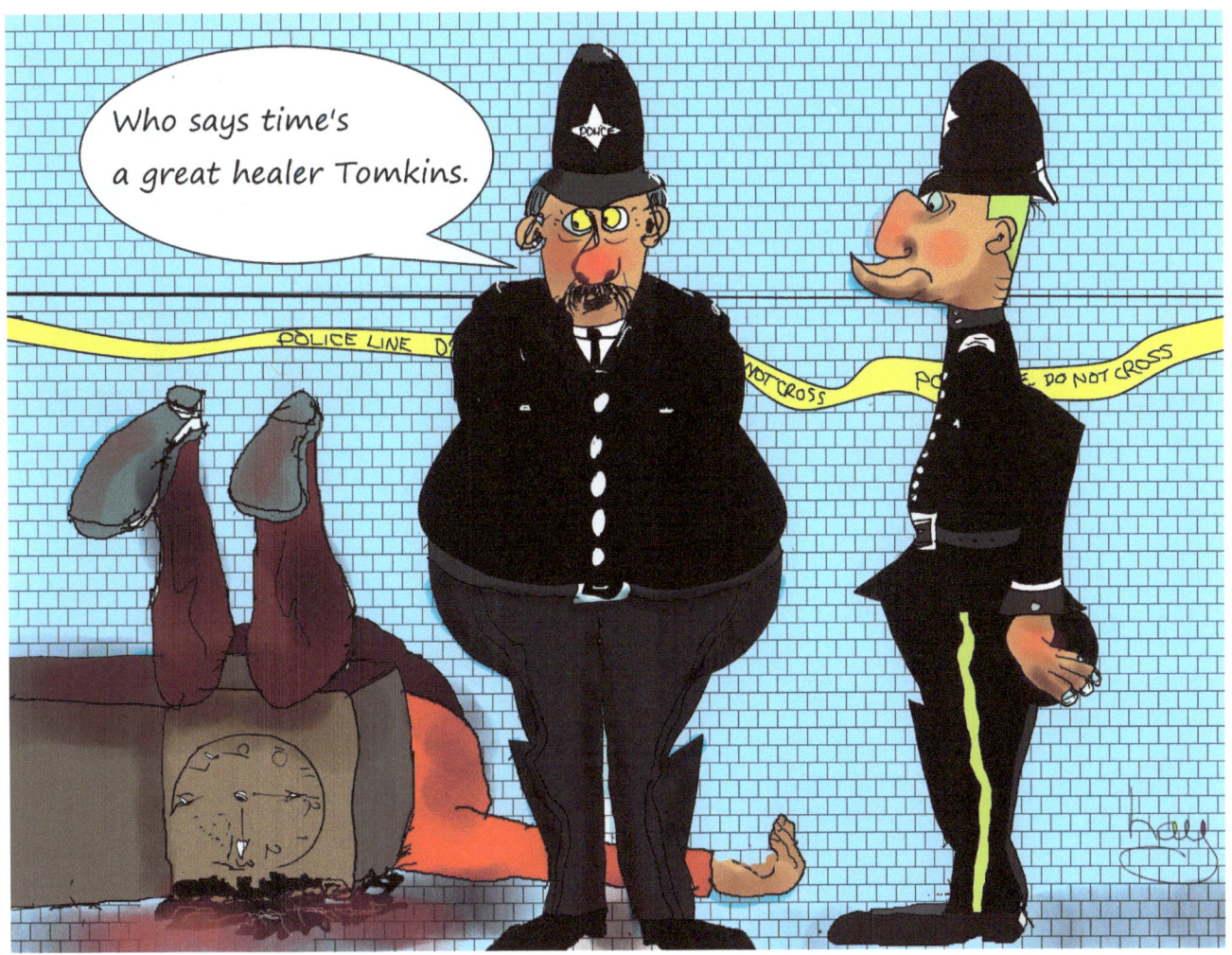

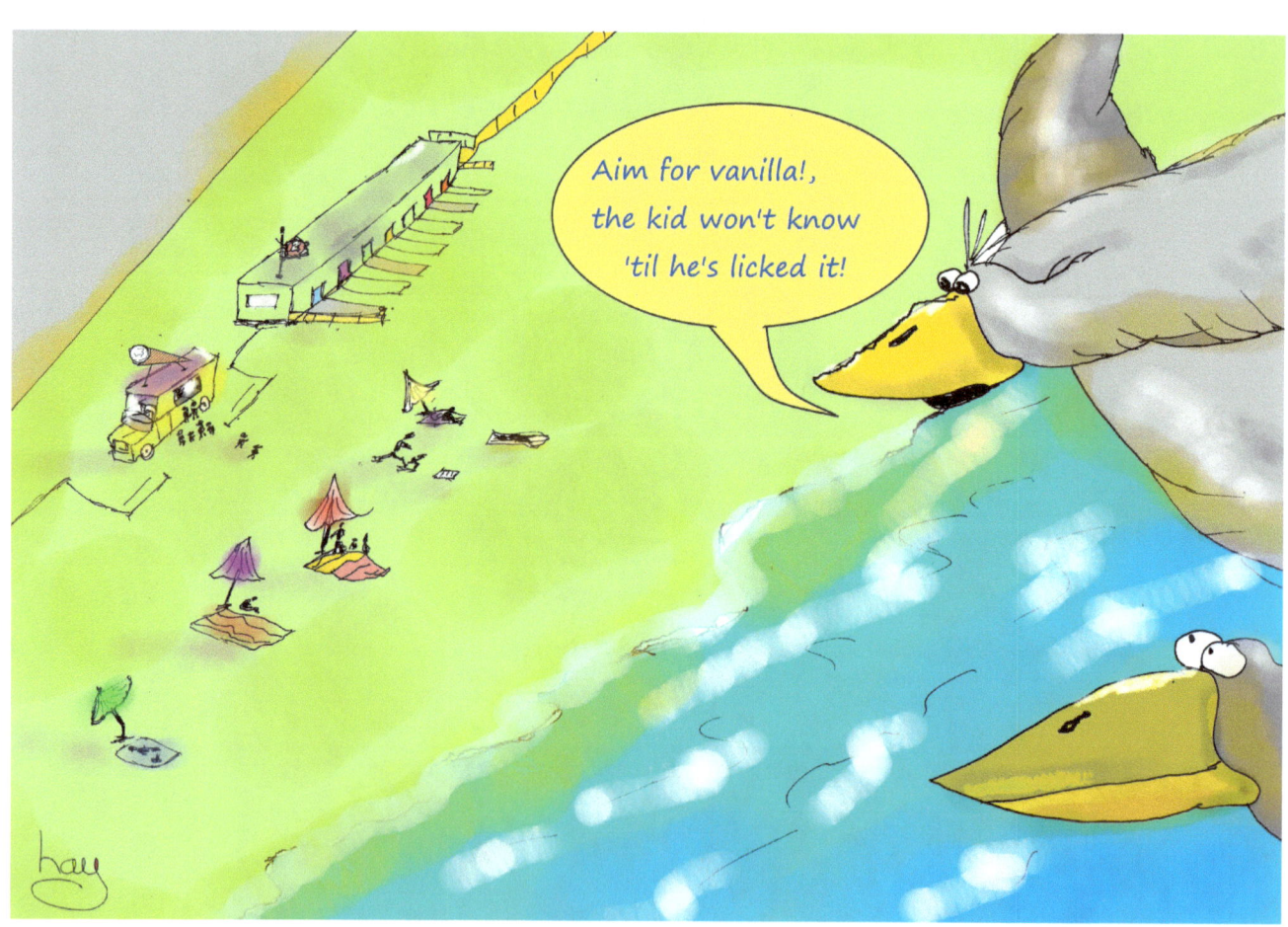

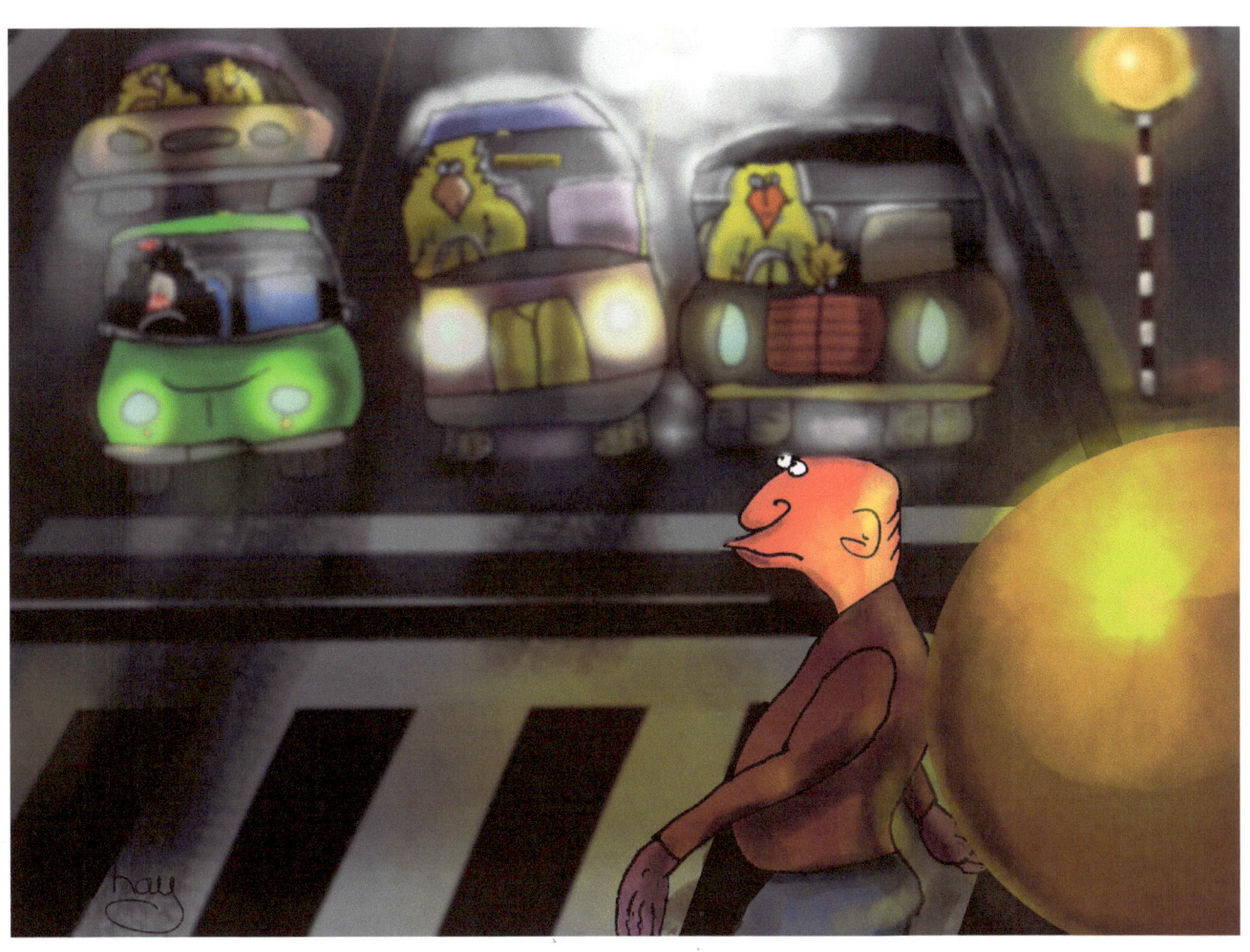

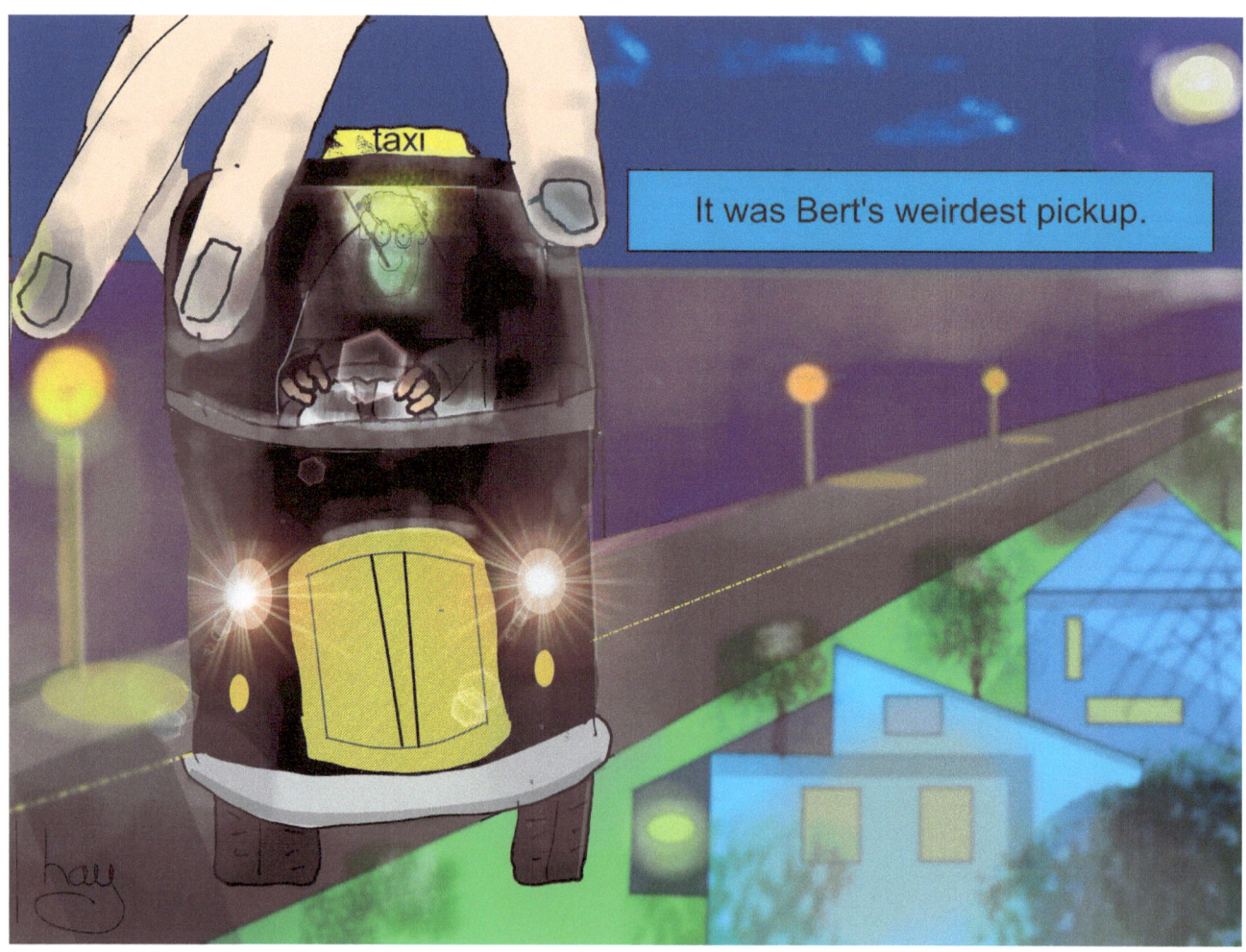

It was Bert's weirdest pickup.

Sidney felt an inexplicable bond with his brother's parrot.

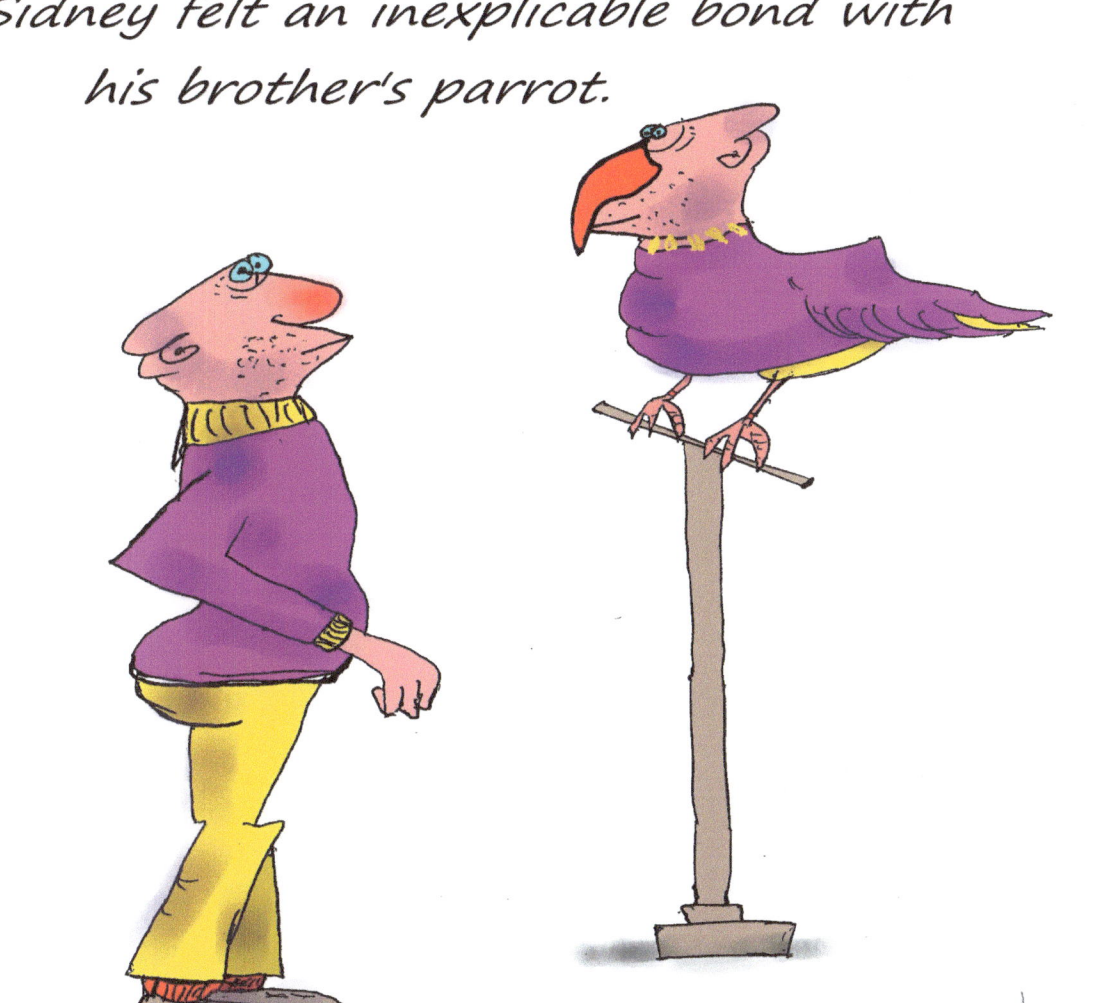

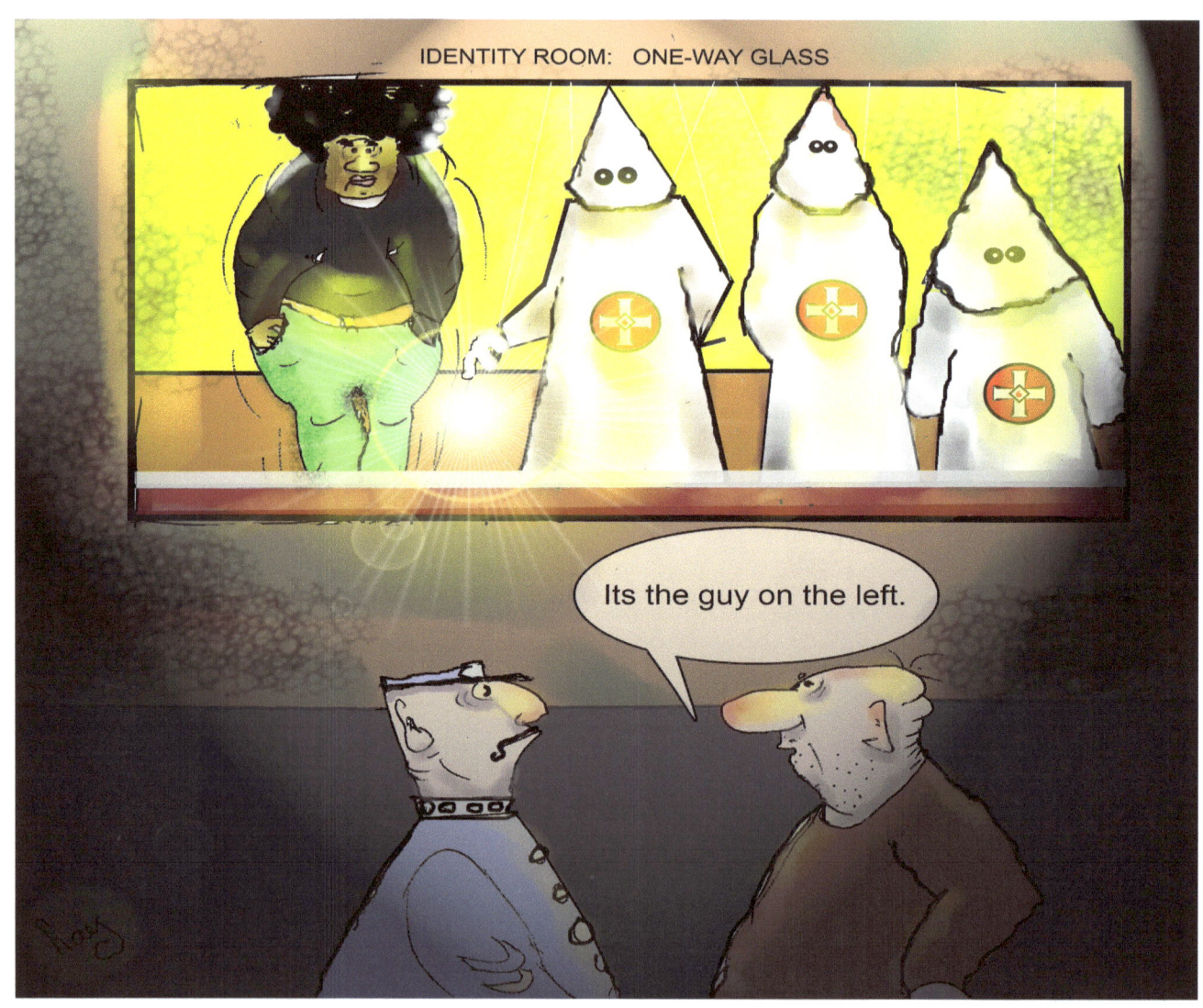

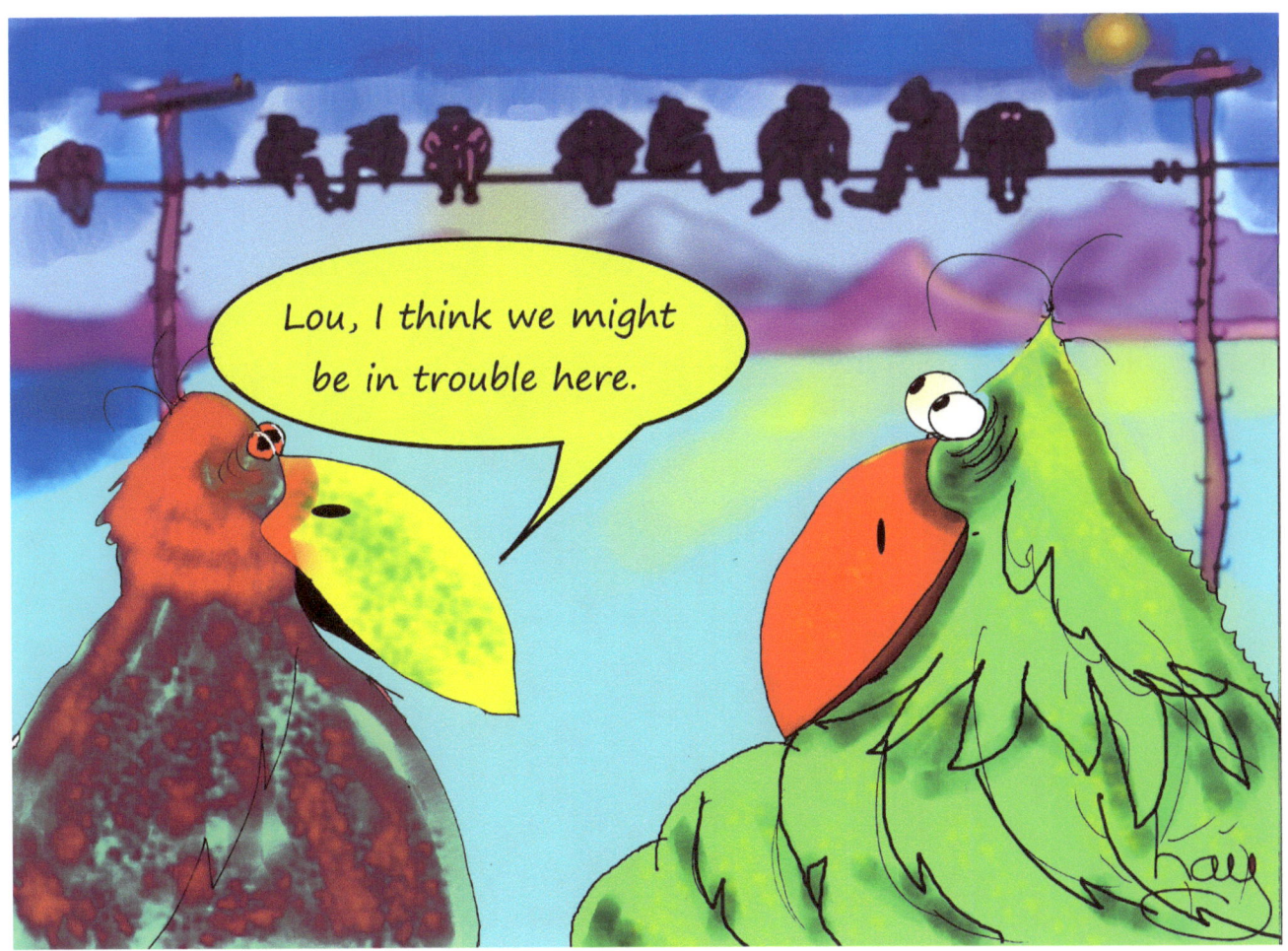

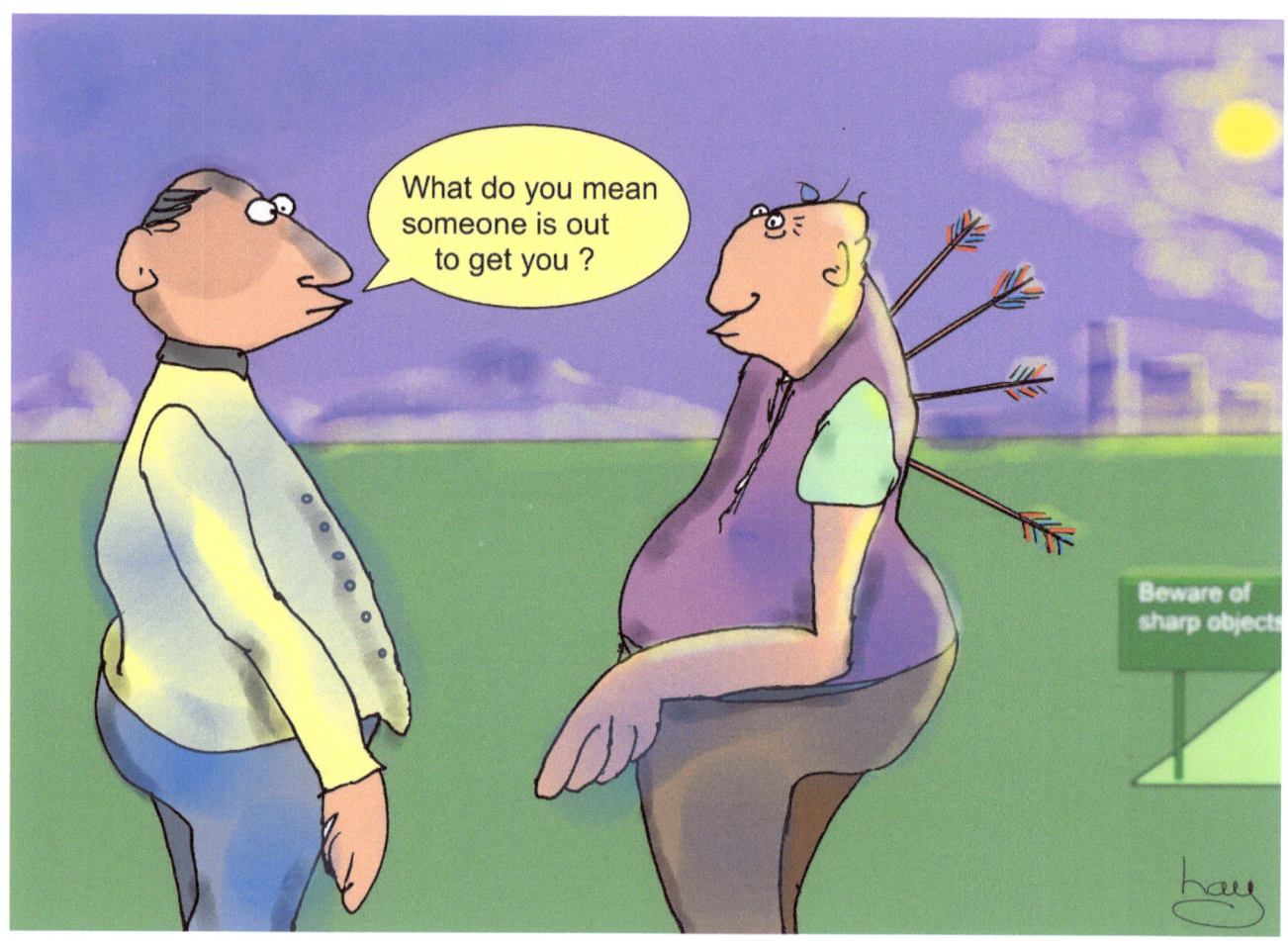

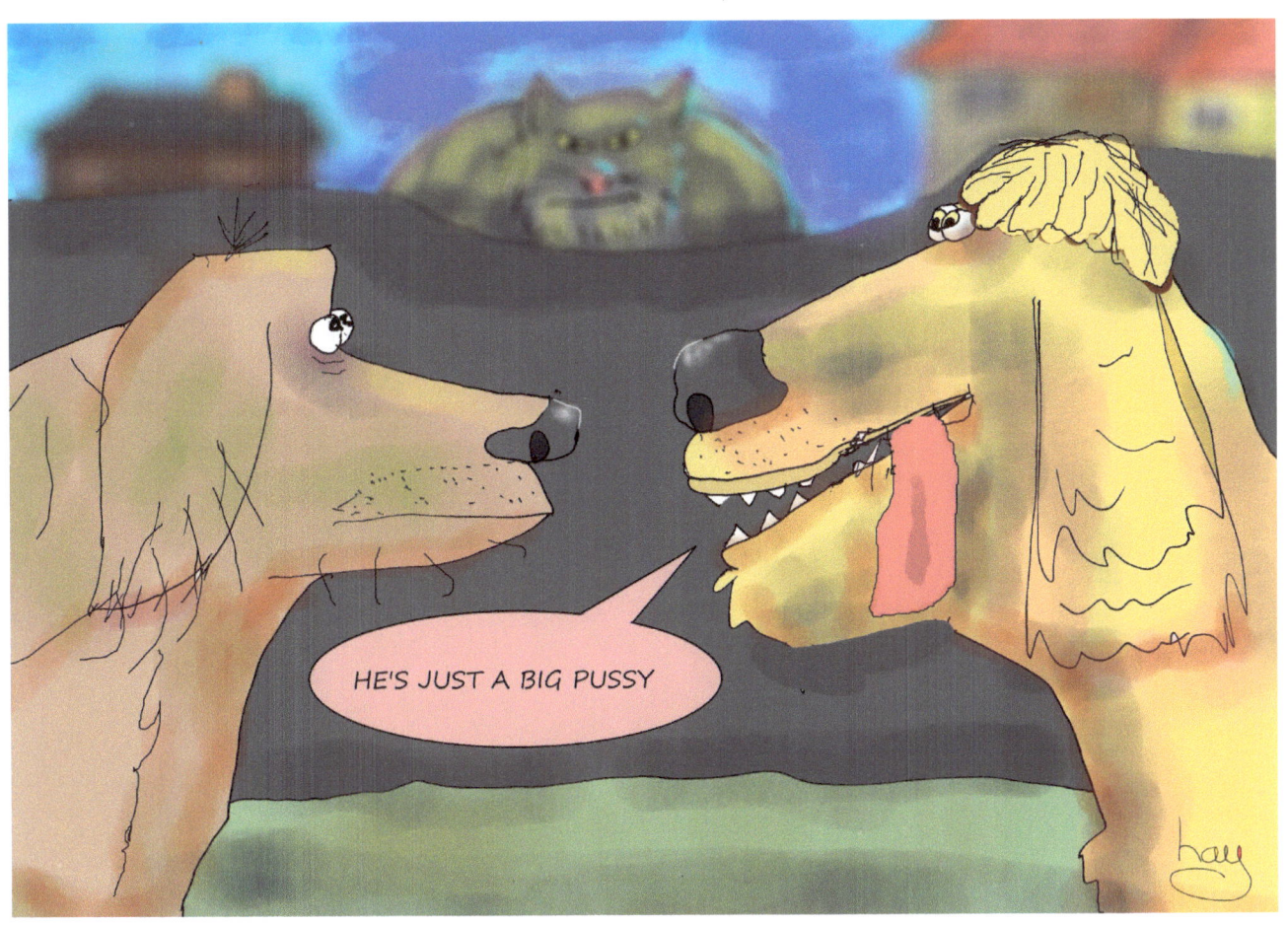

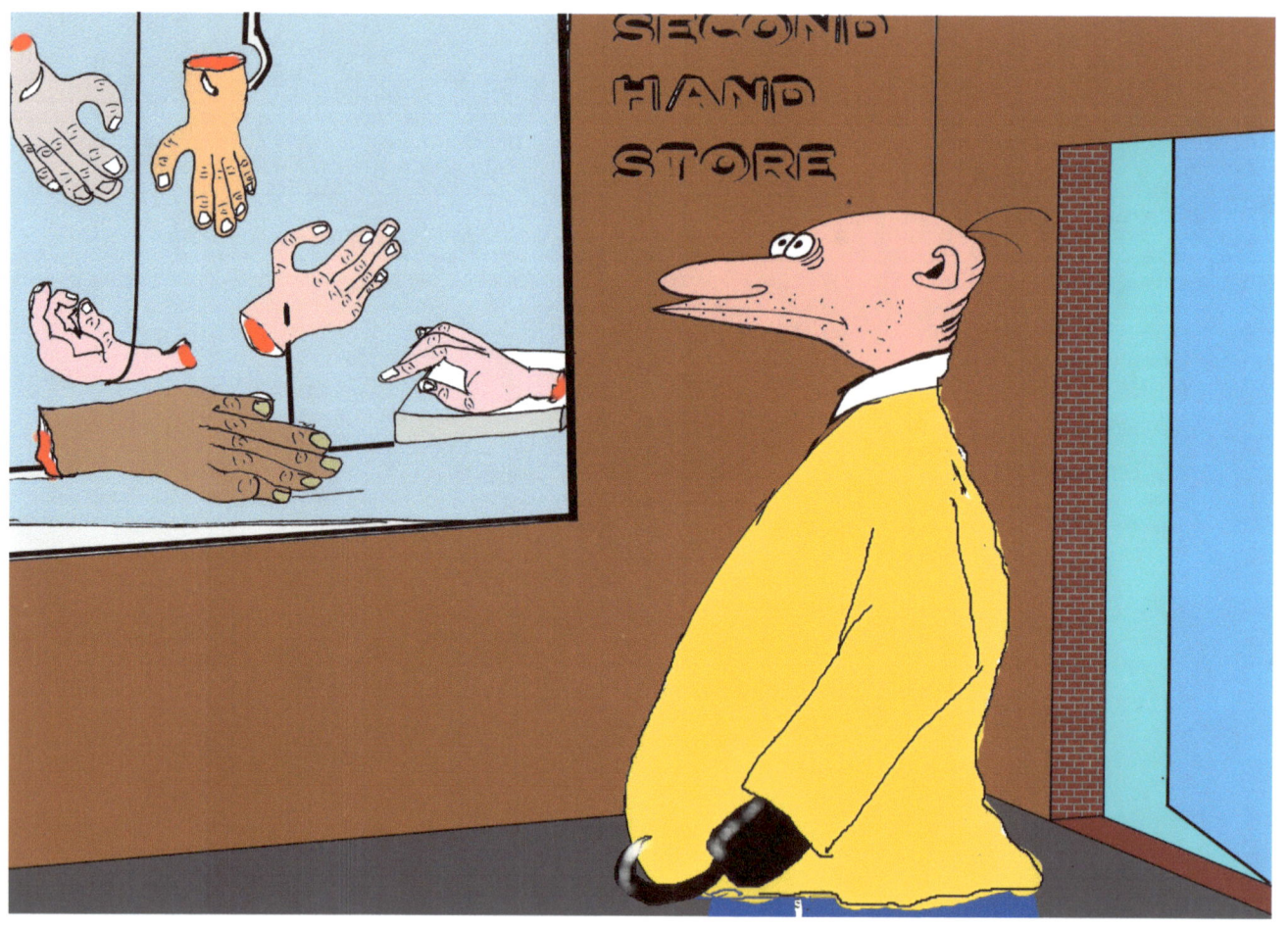

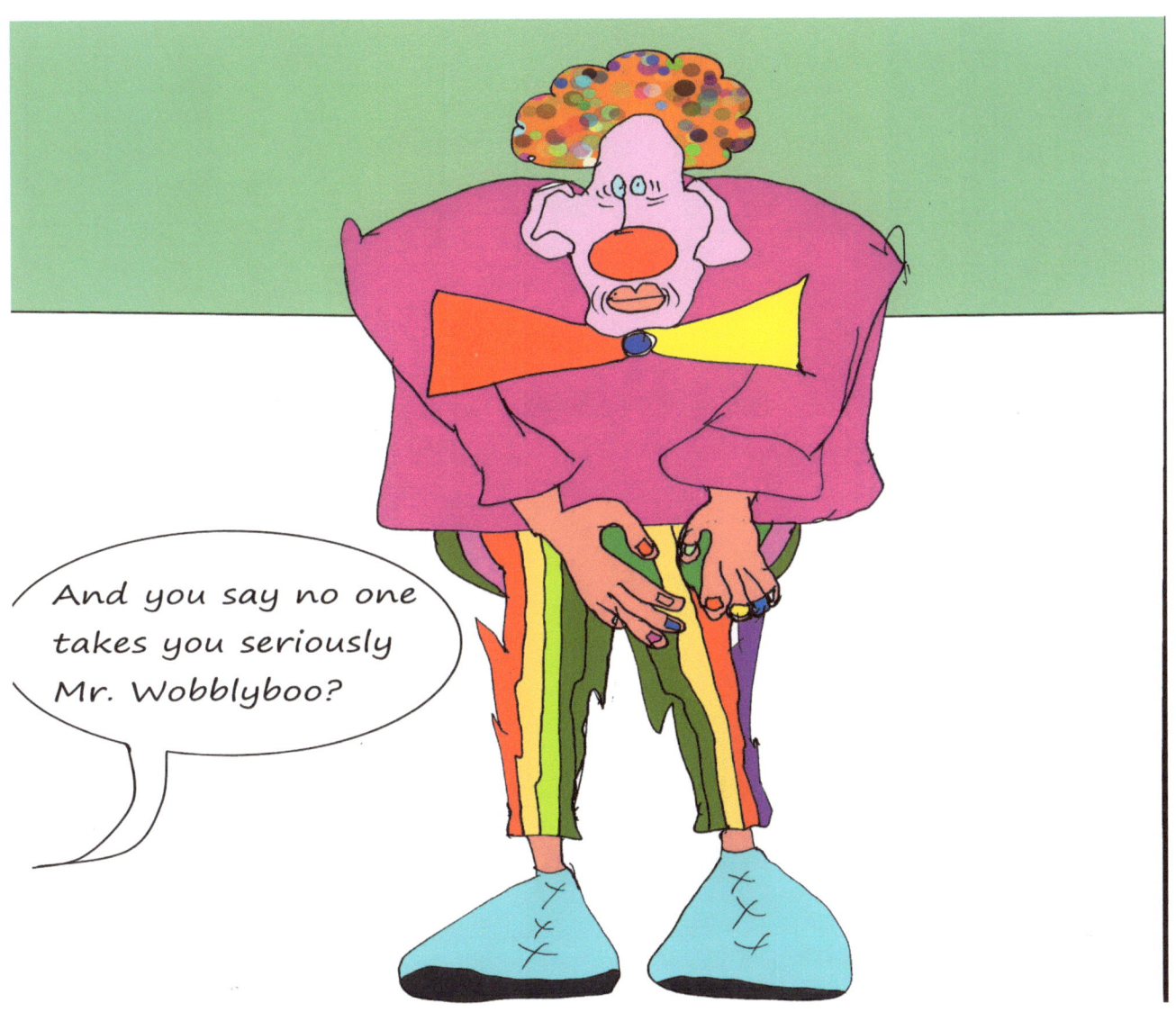

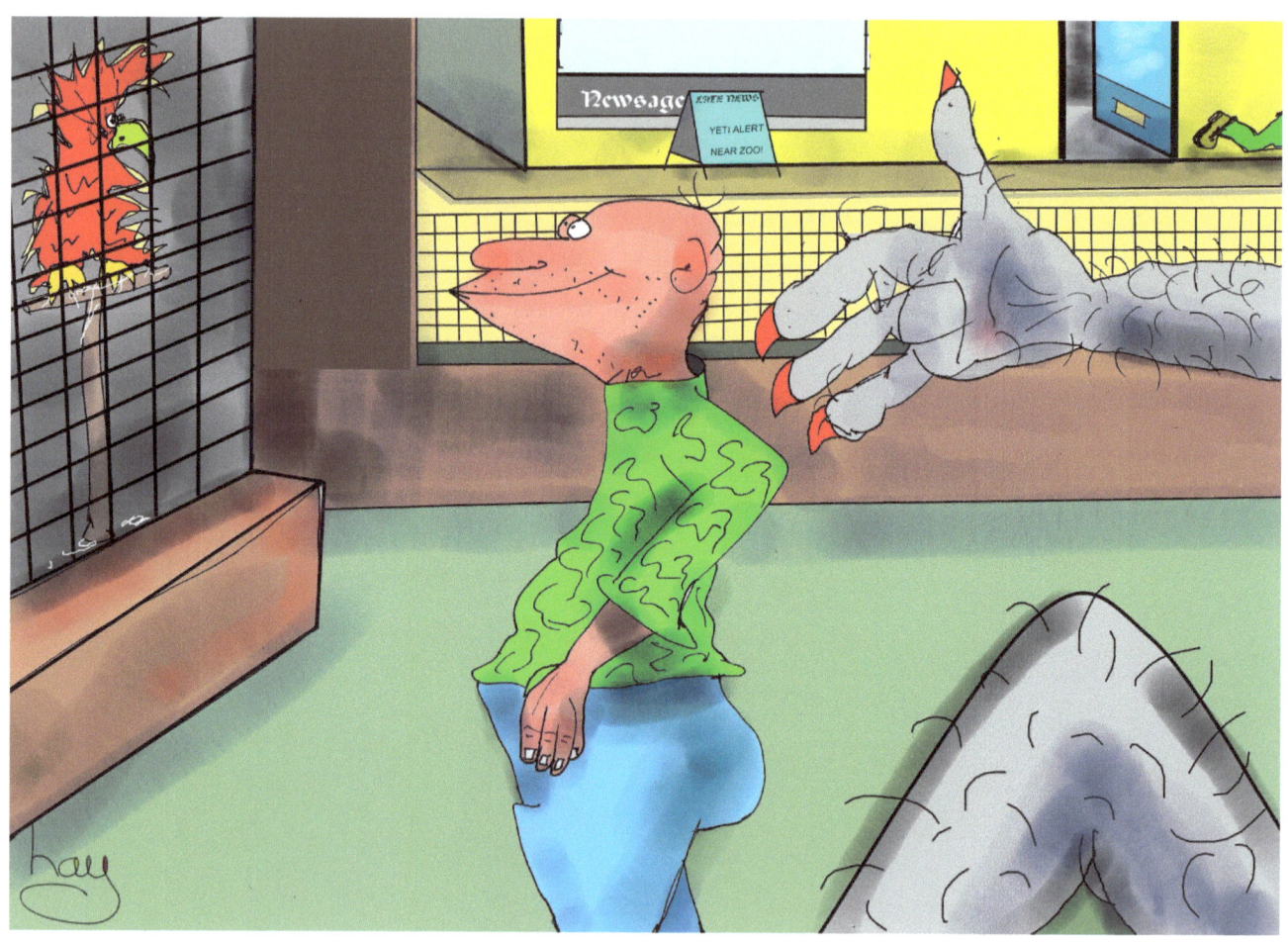

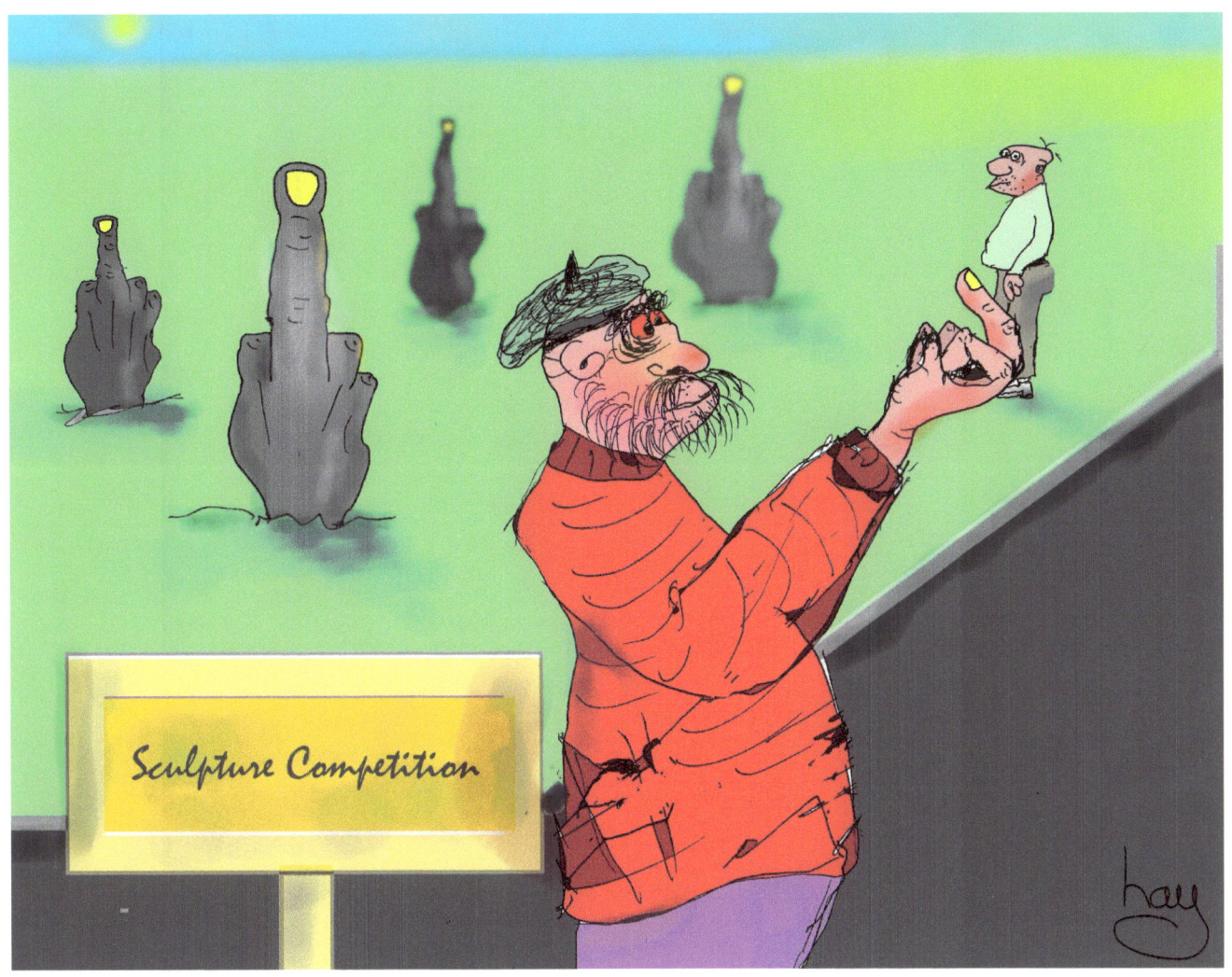

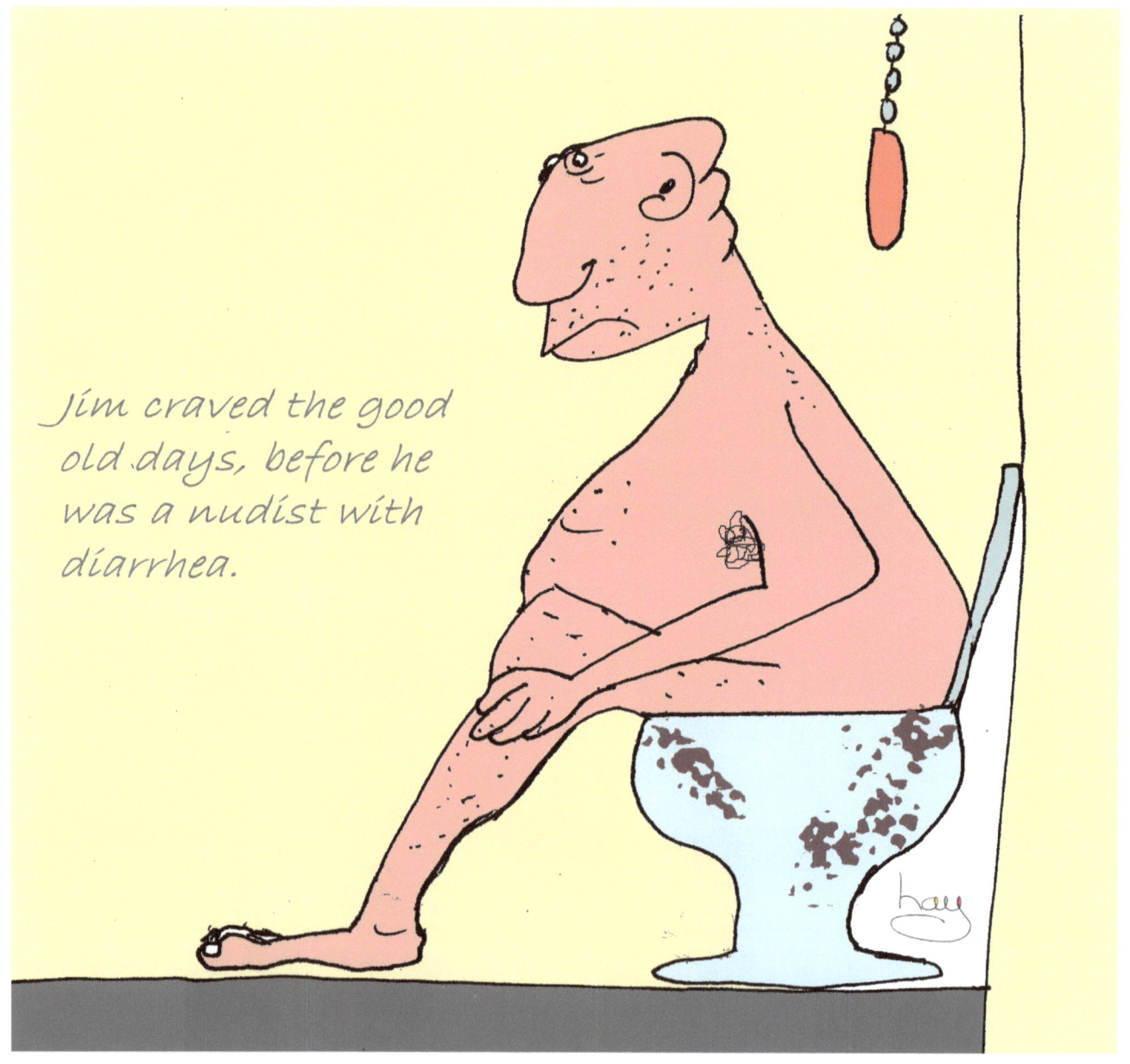

Jim craved the good old days, before he was a nudist with diarrhea.

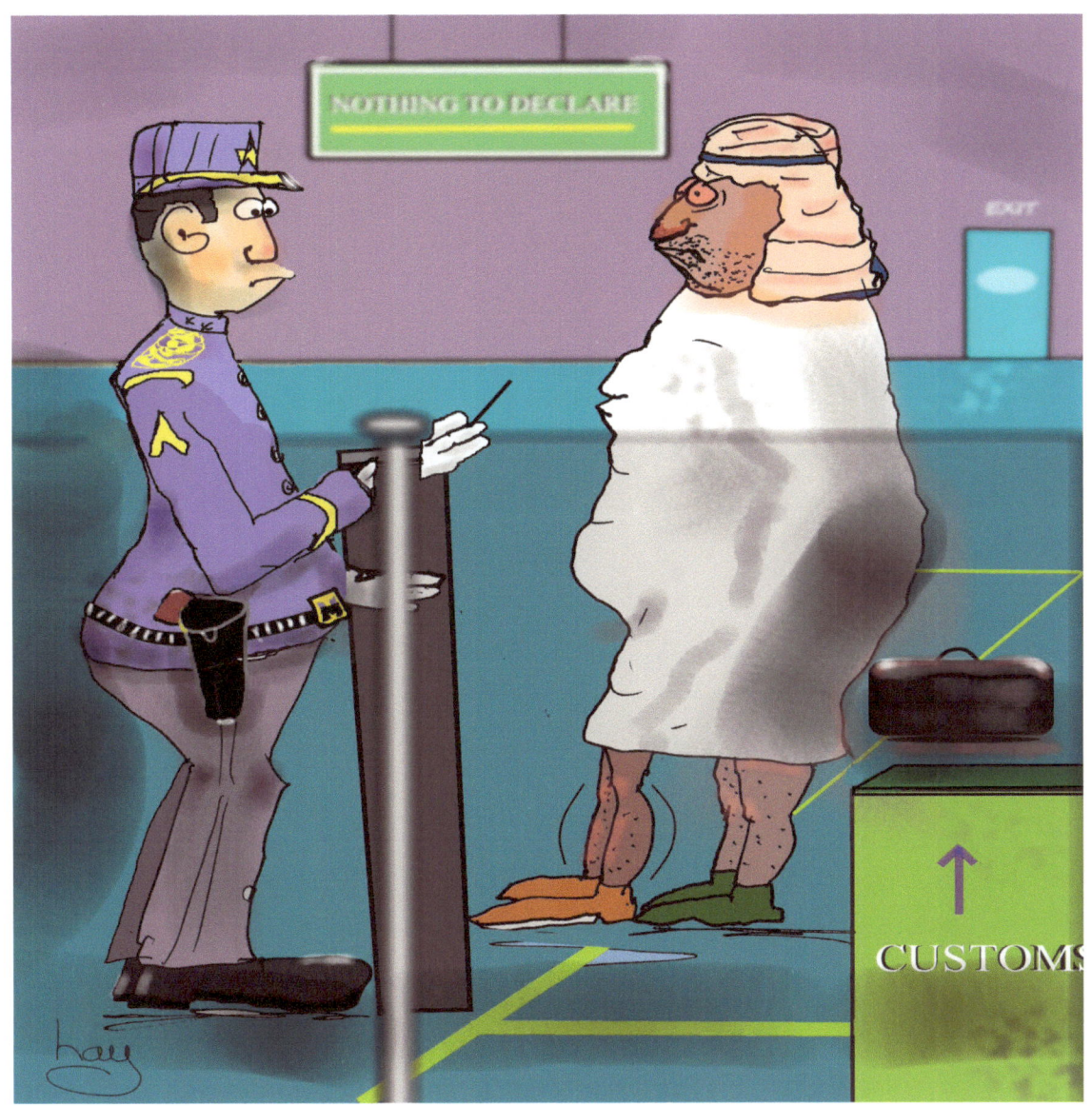

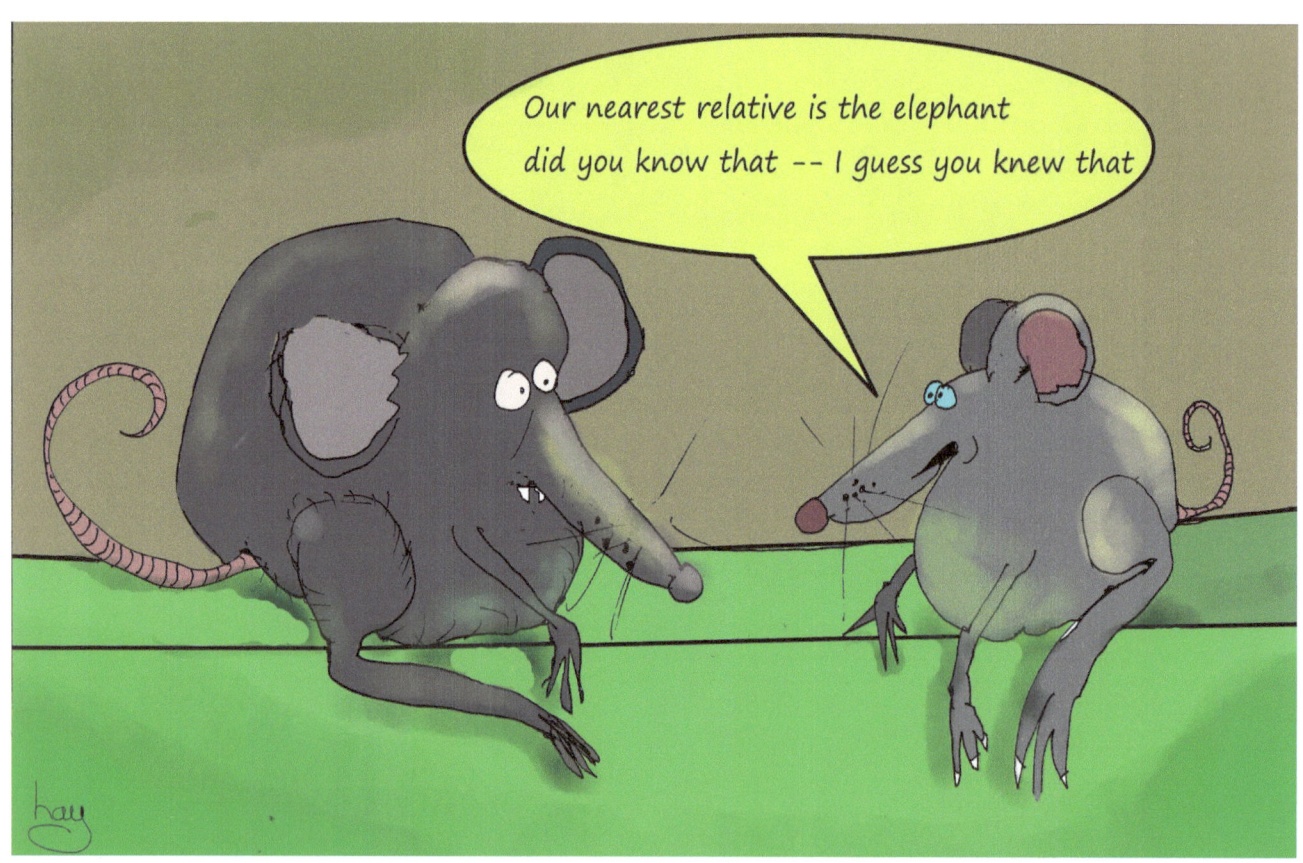

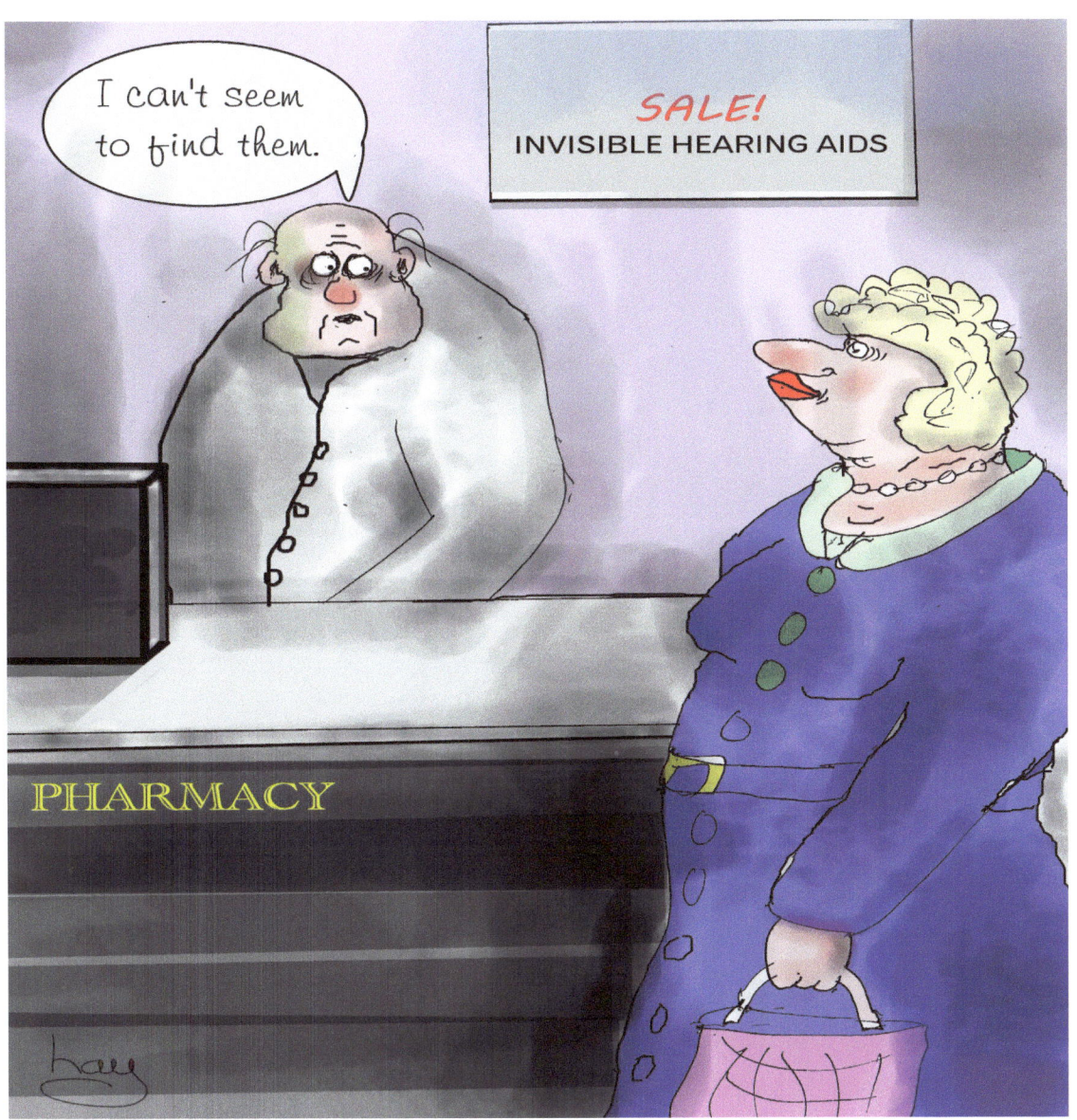

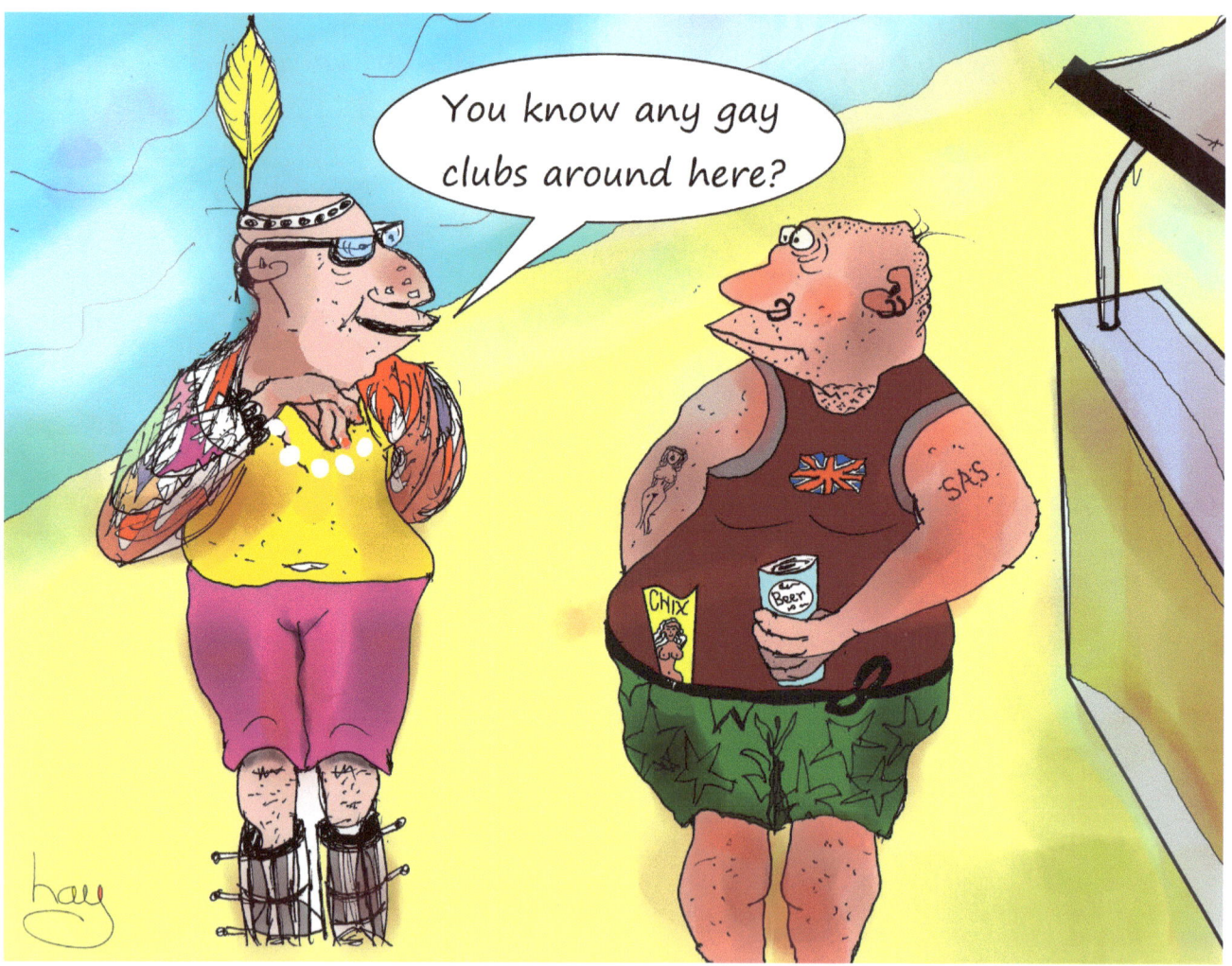

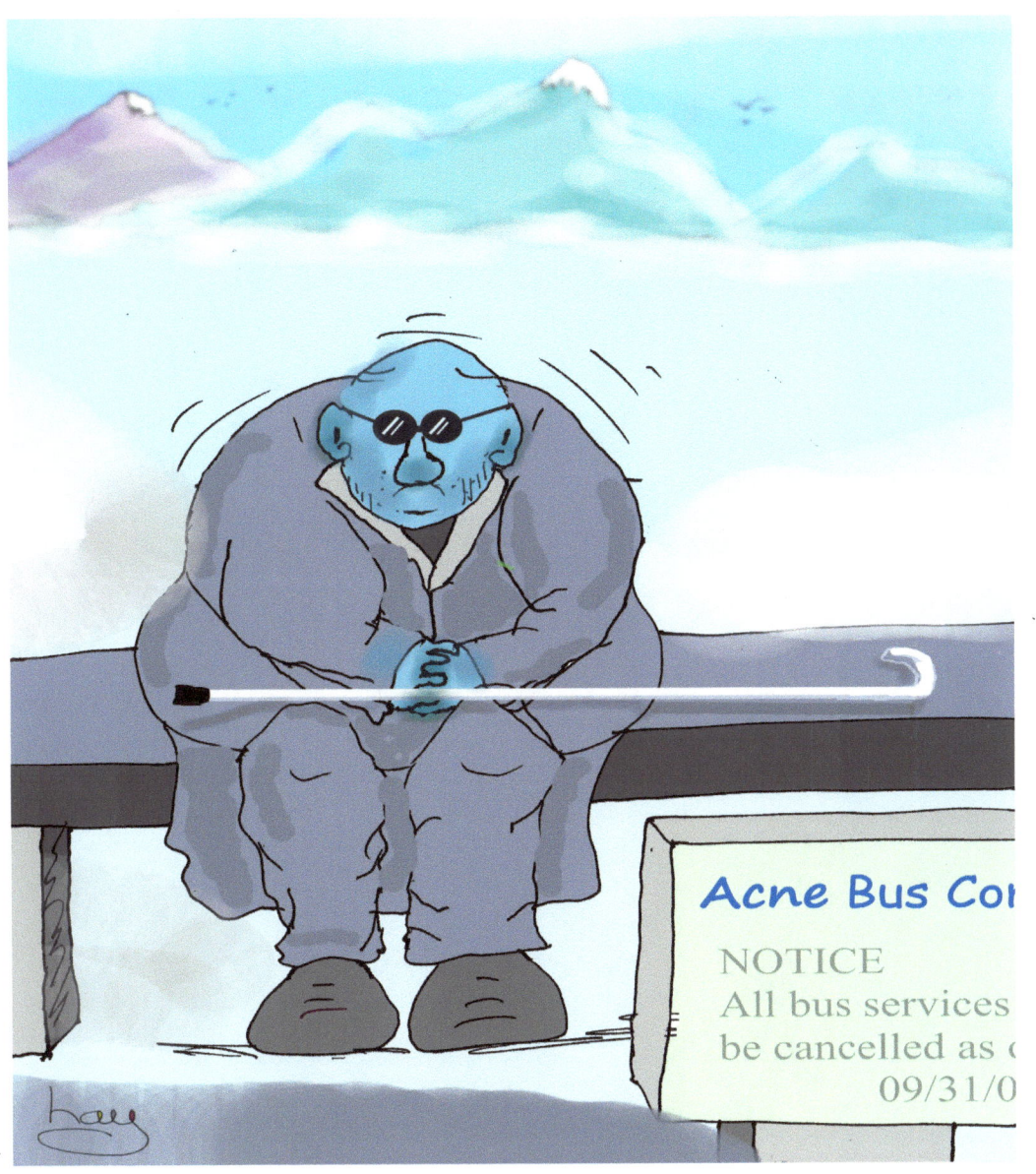

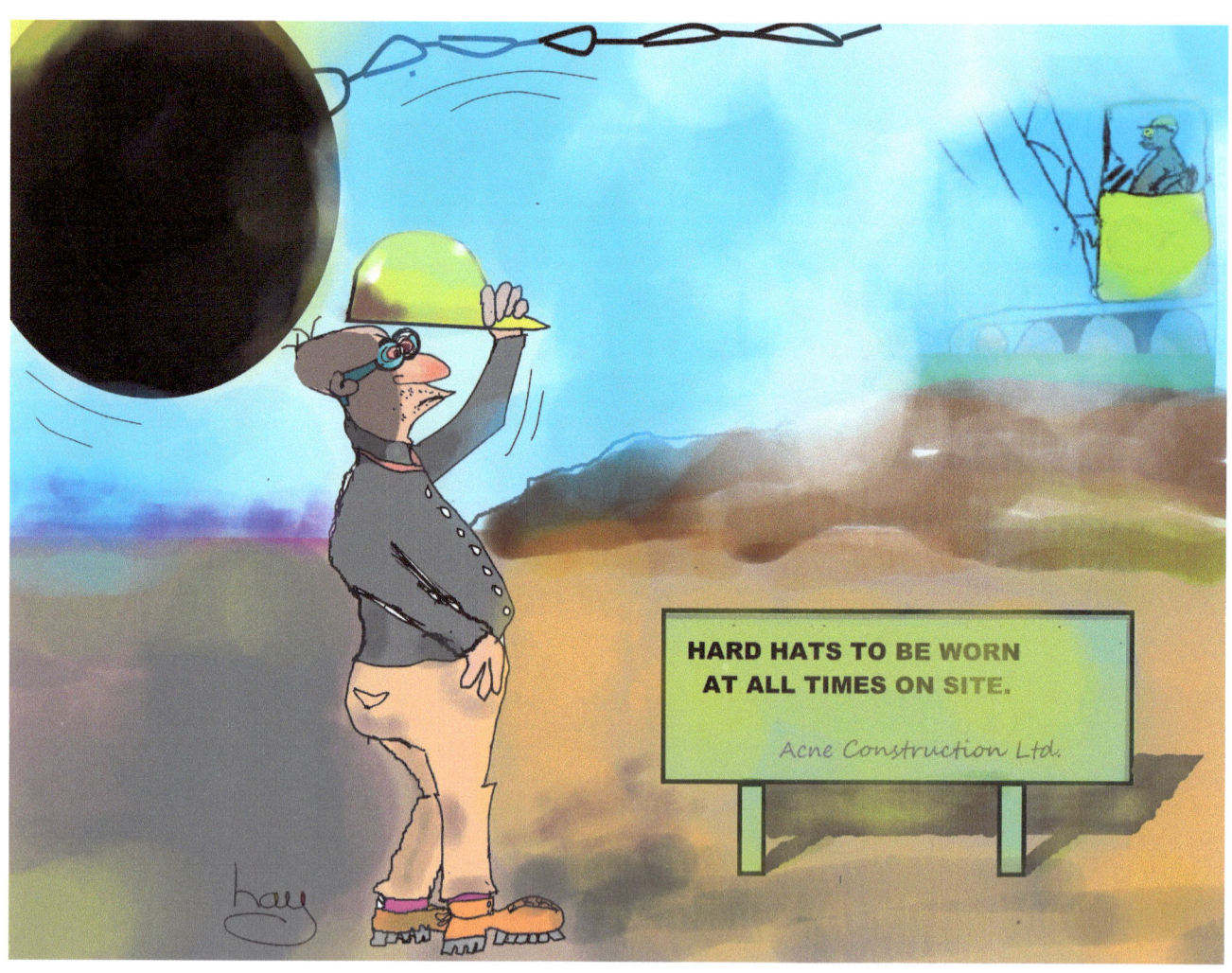

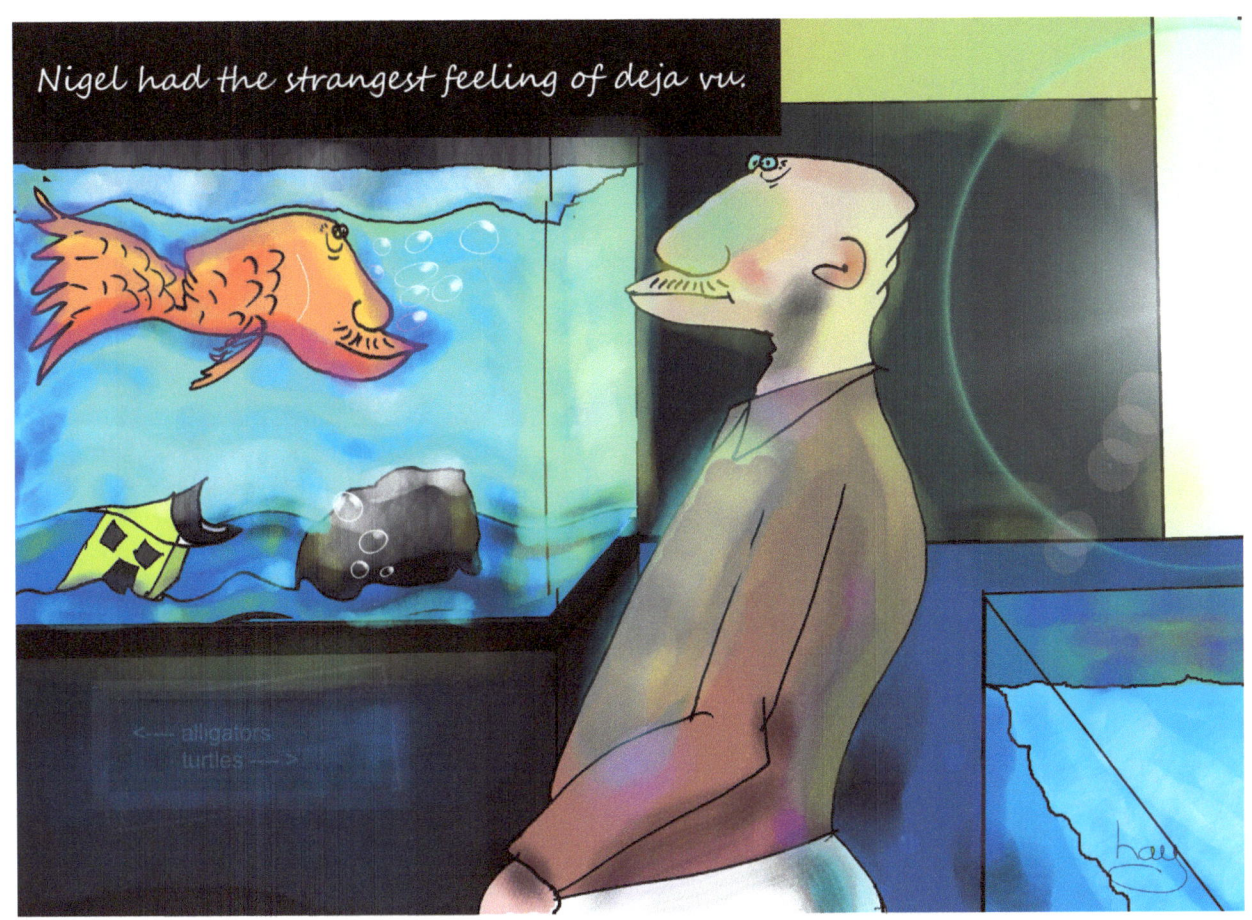

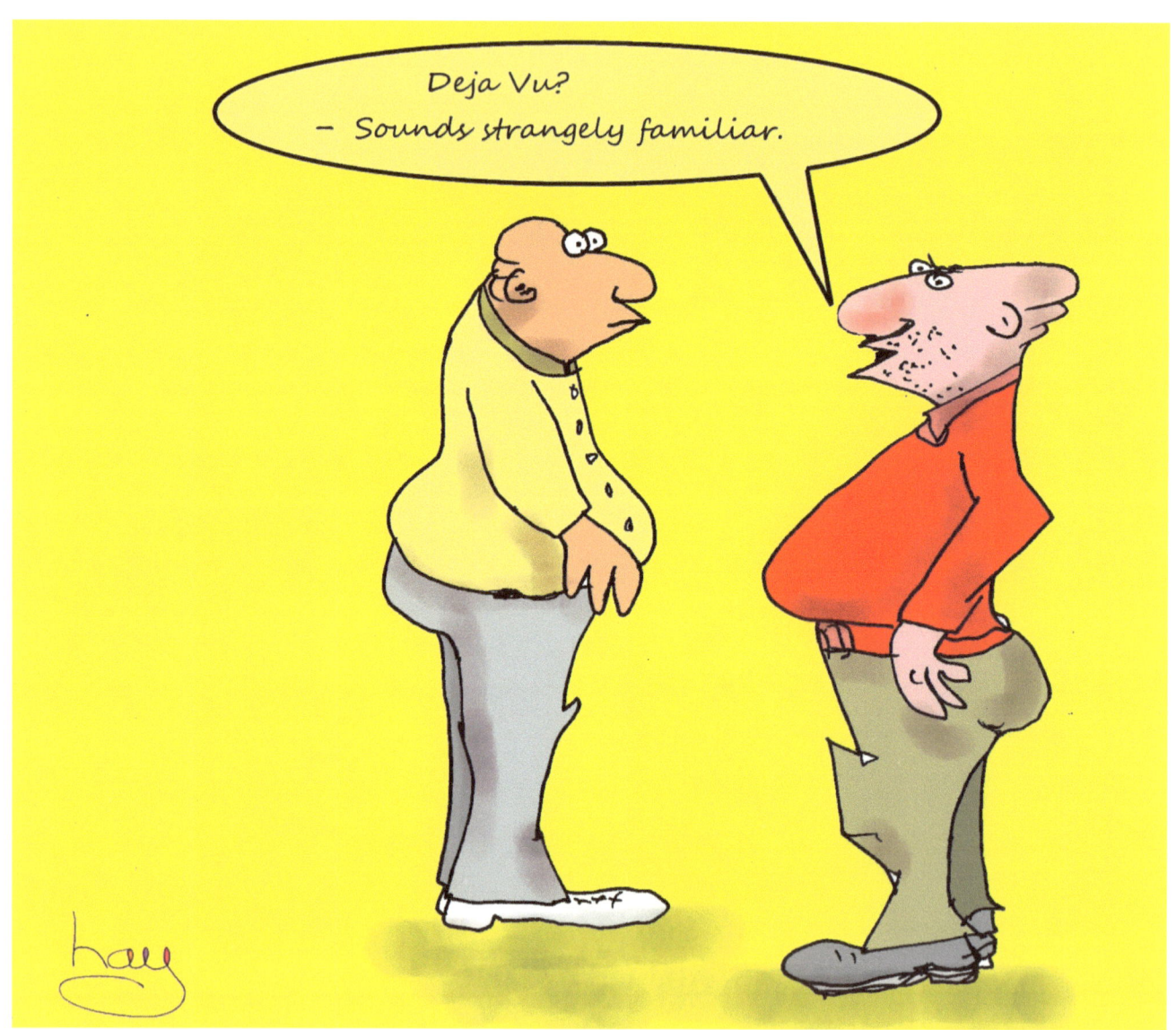

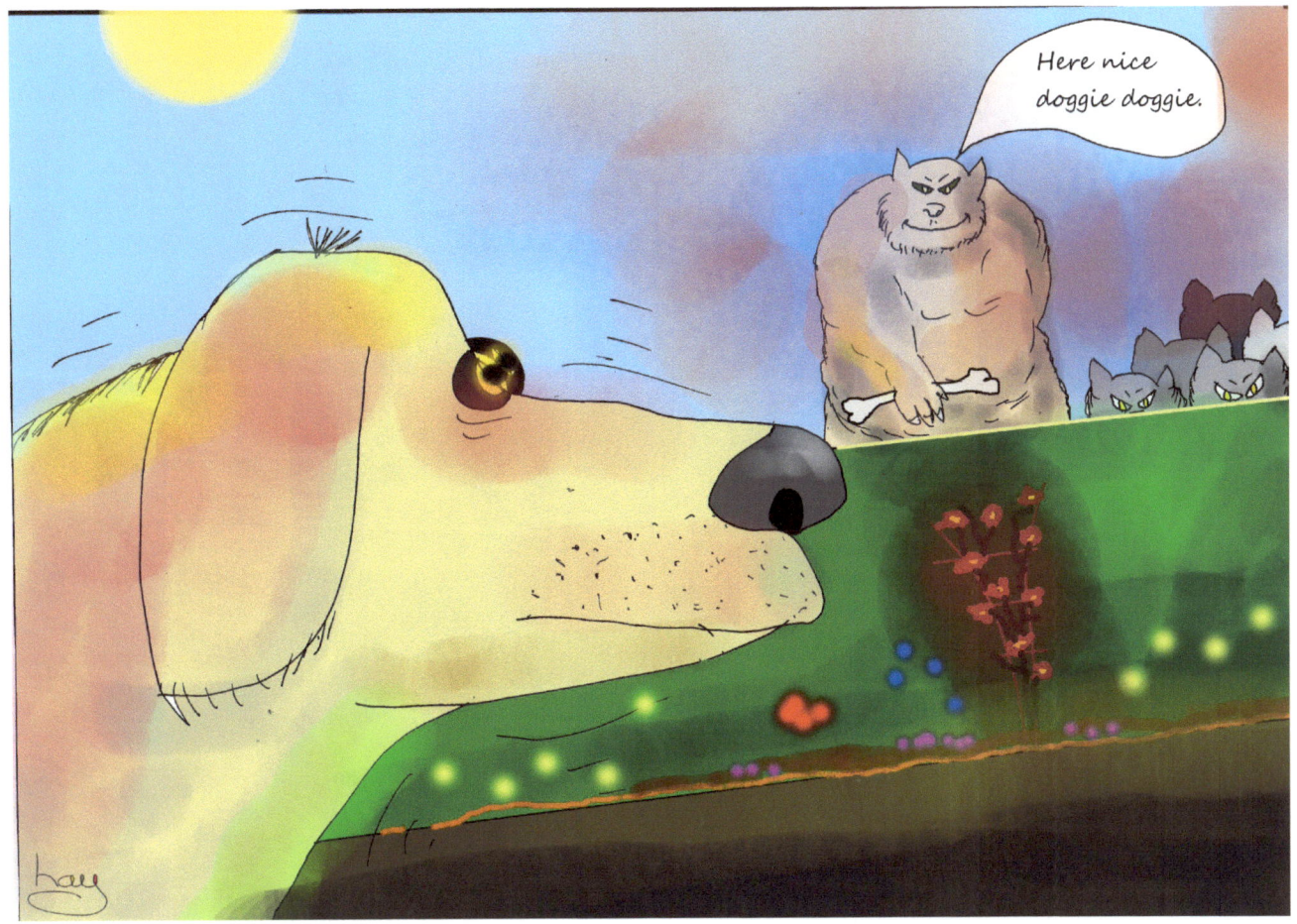

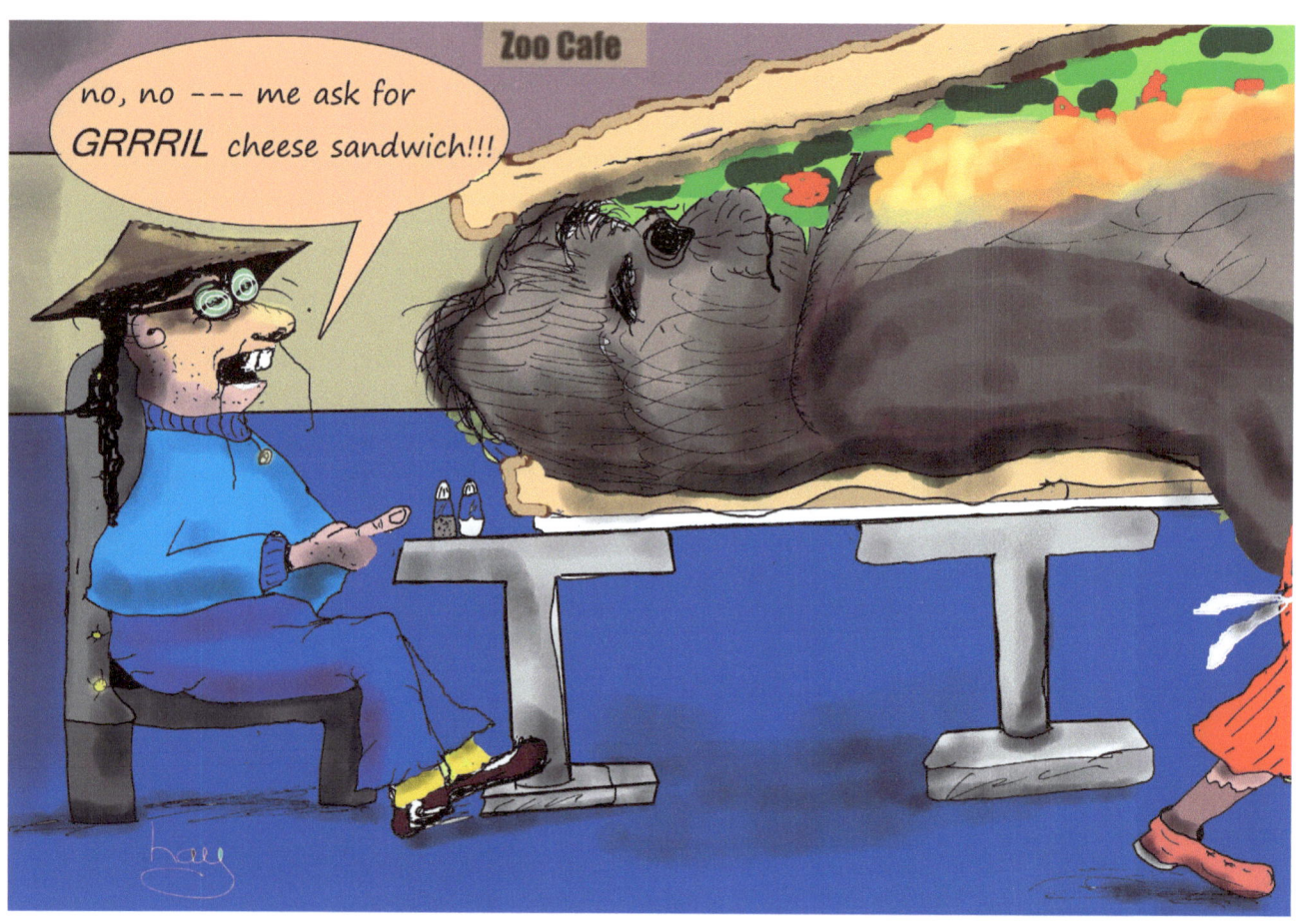

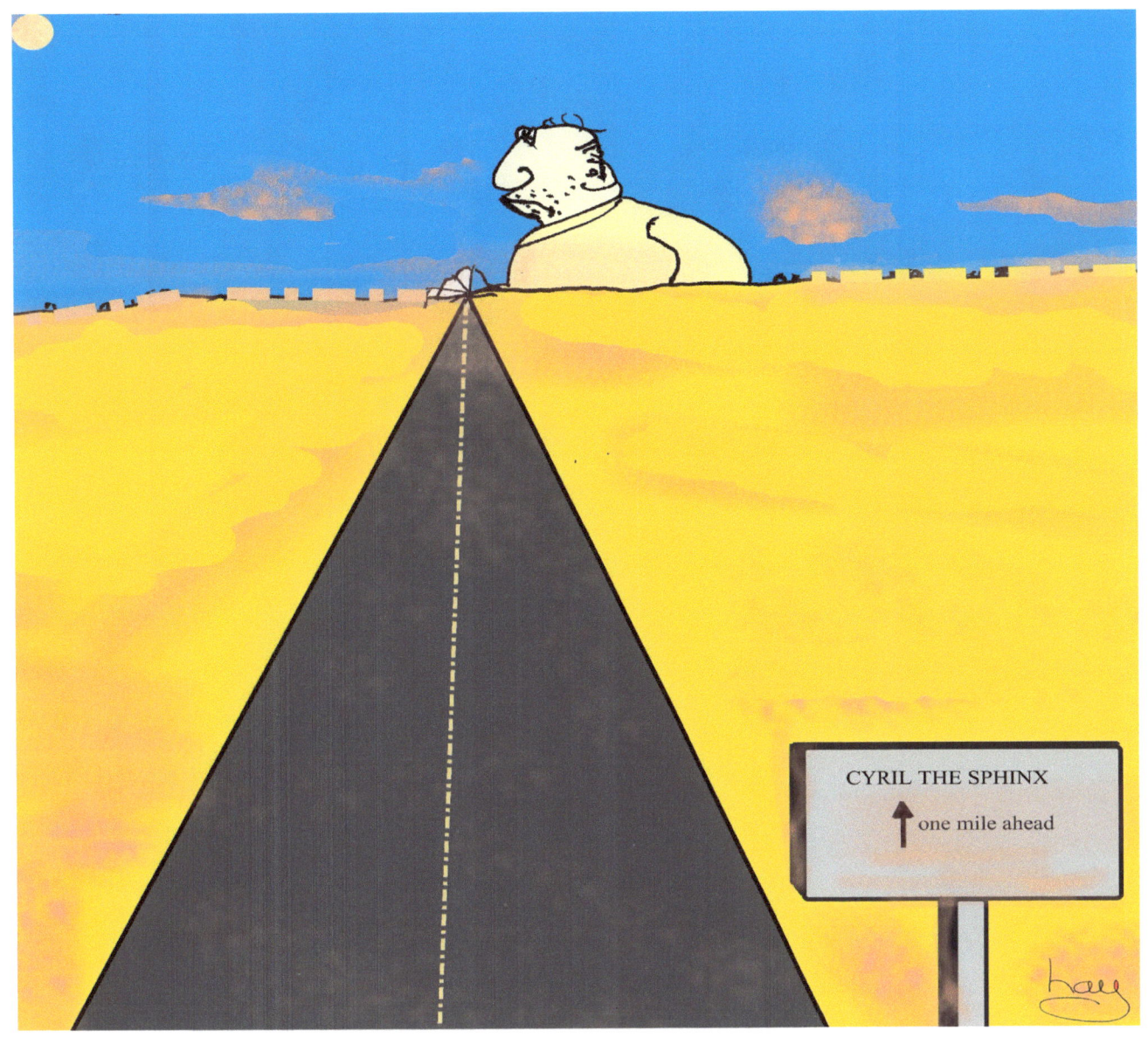

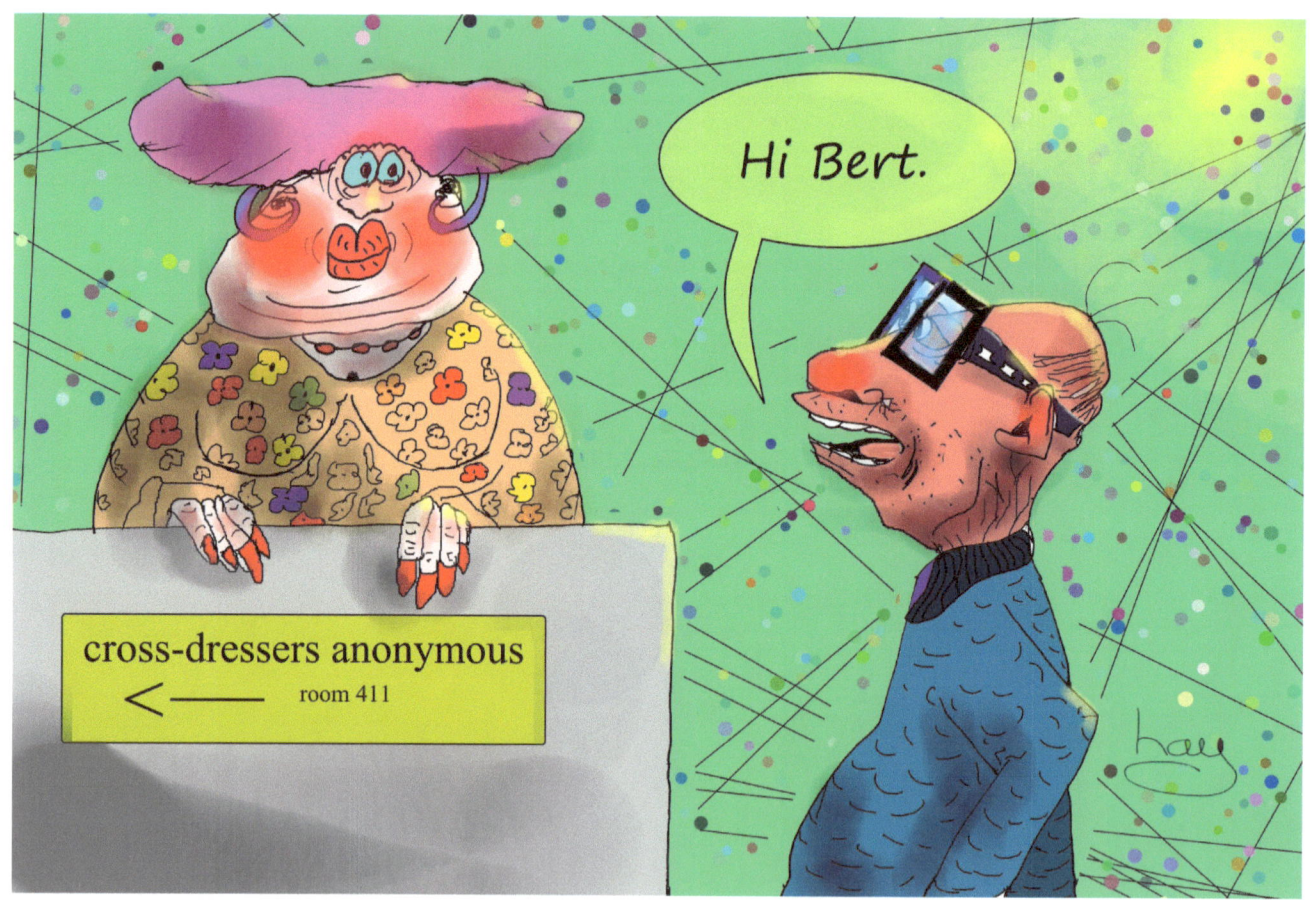

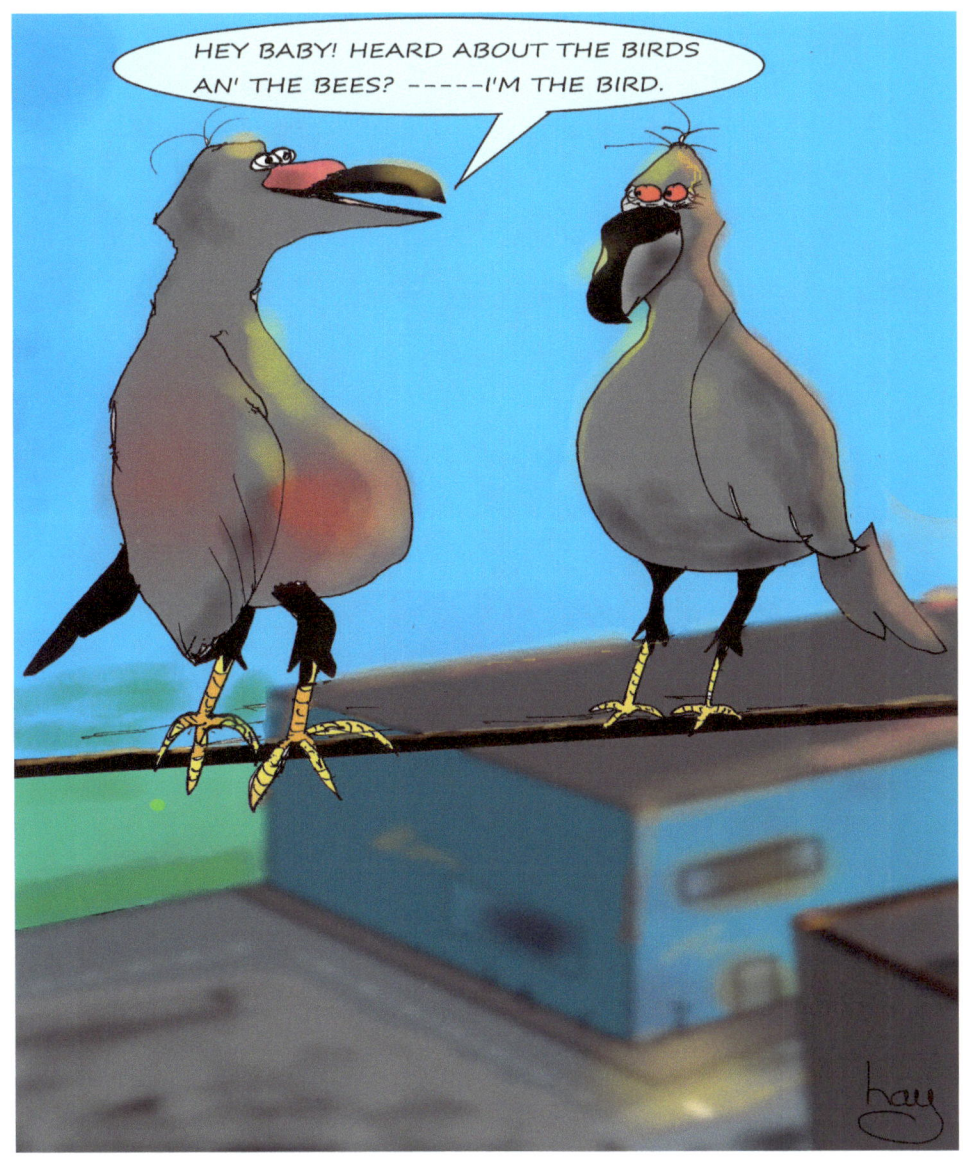

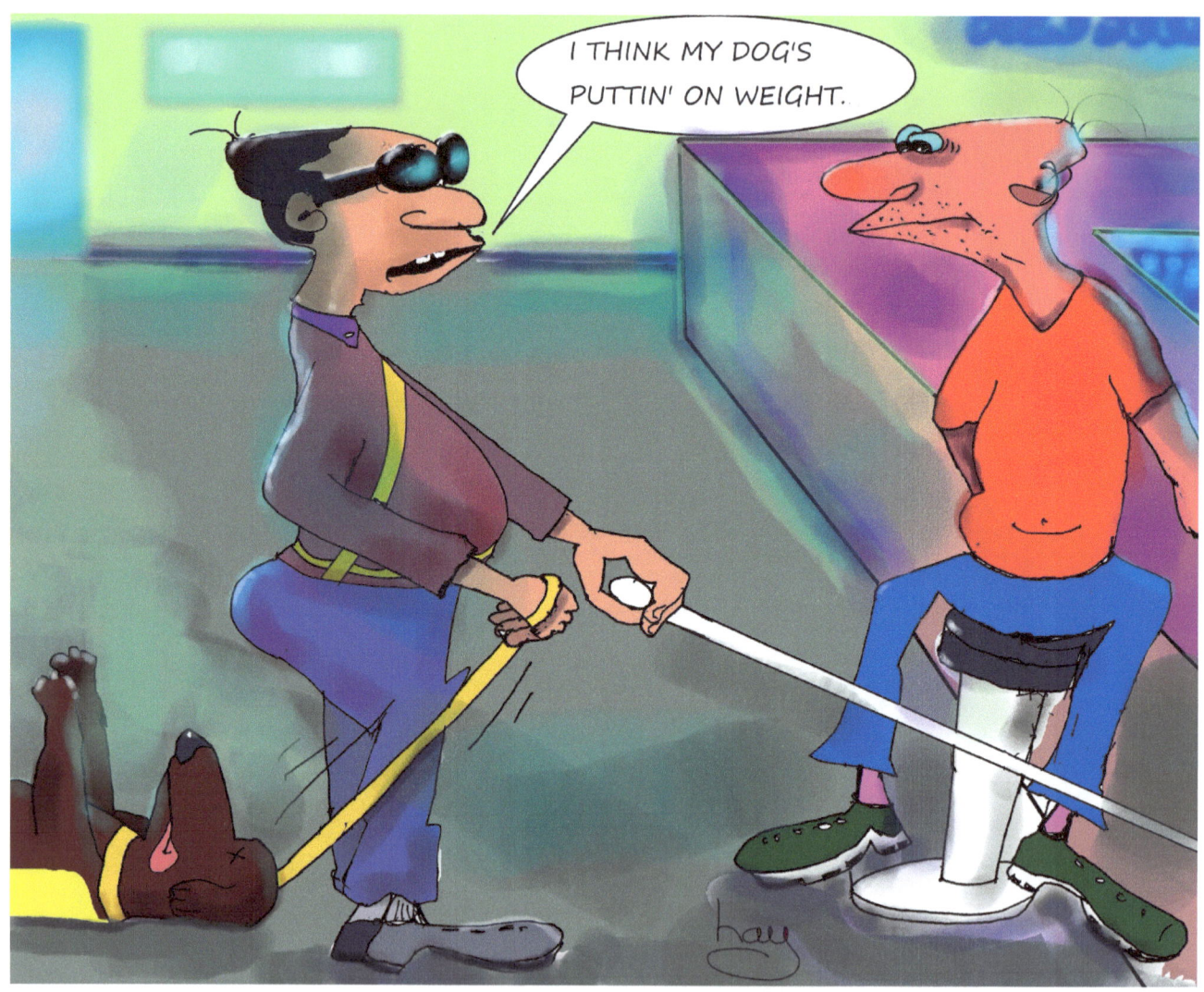

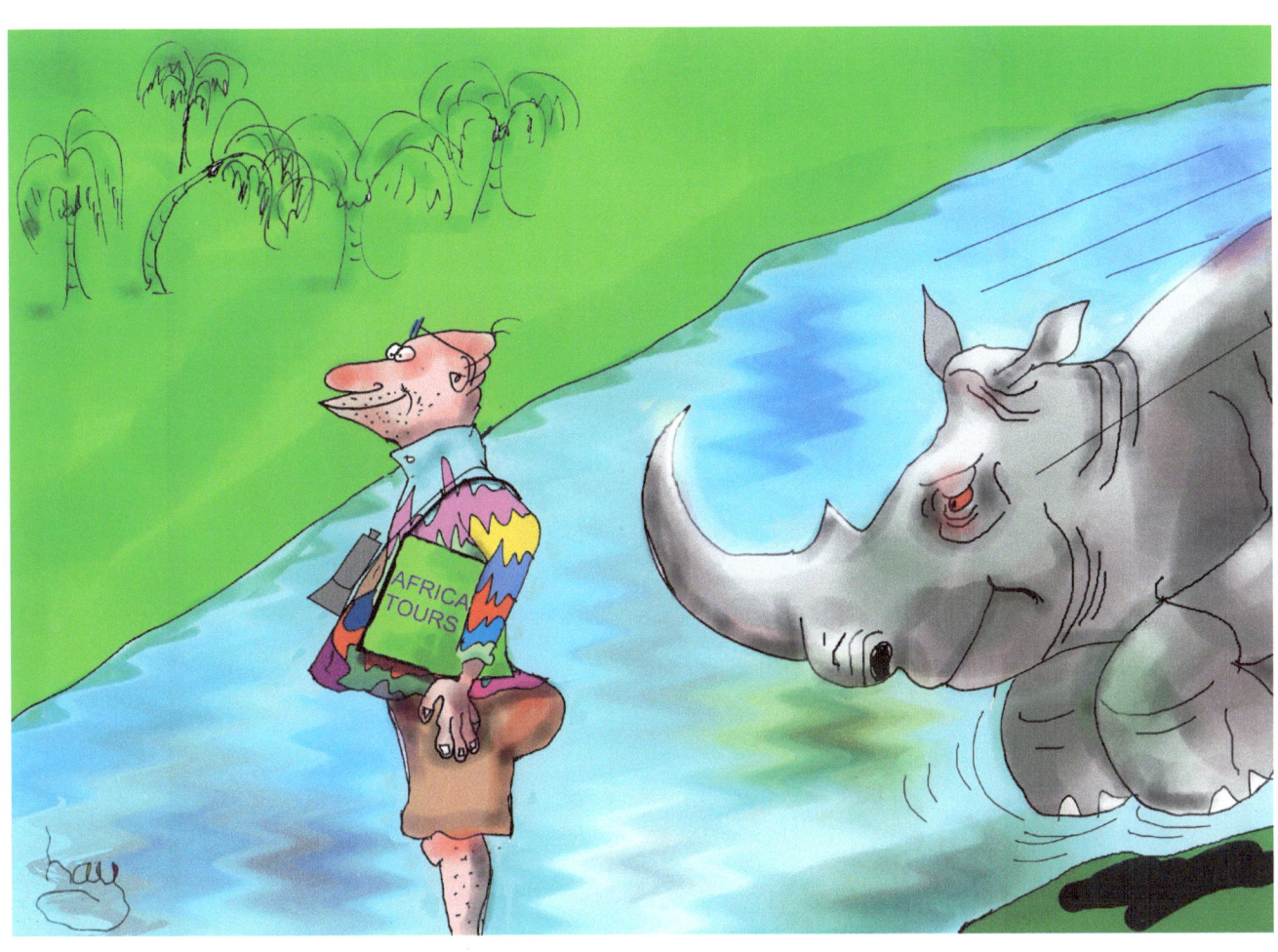

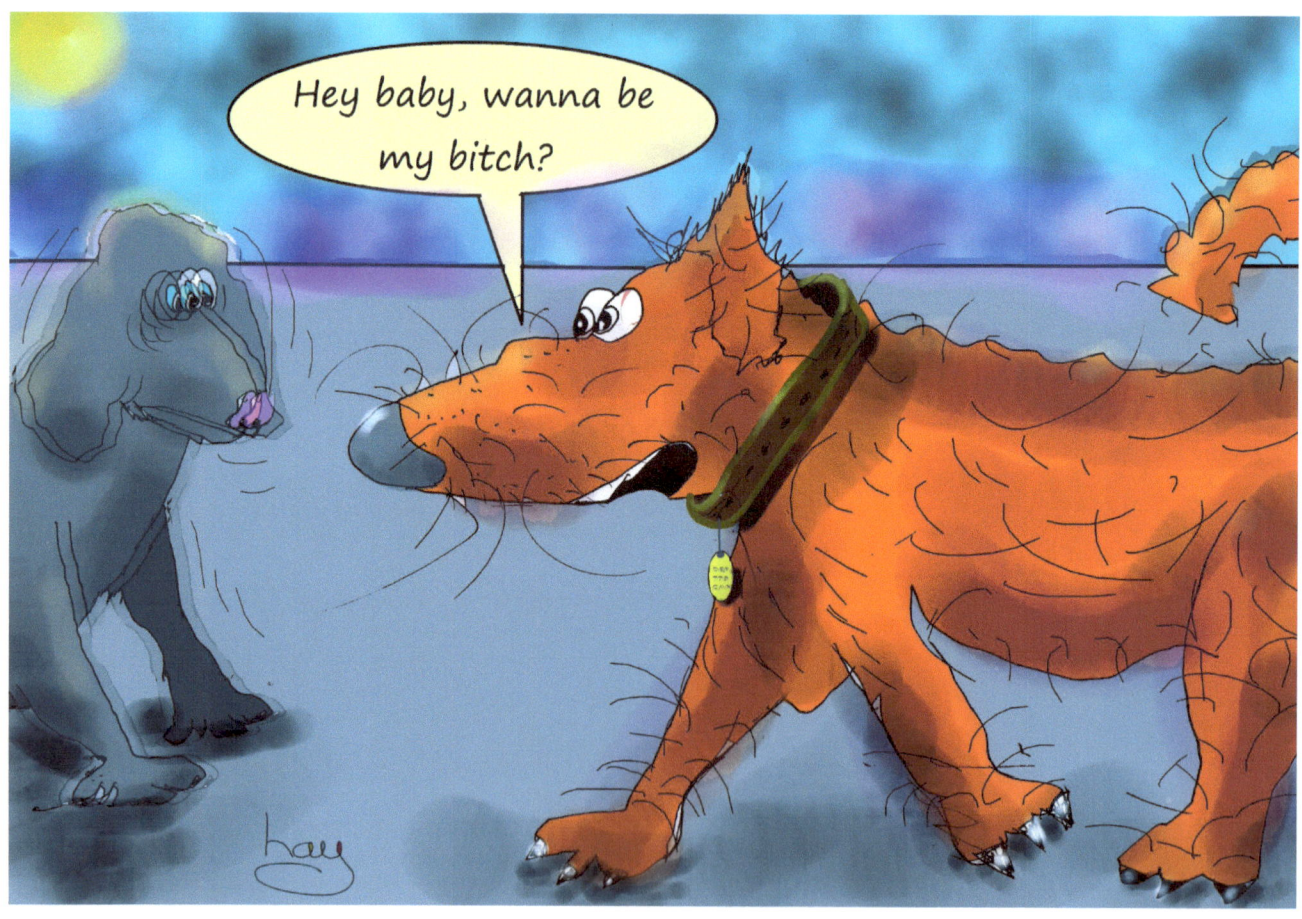

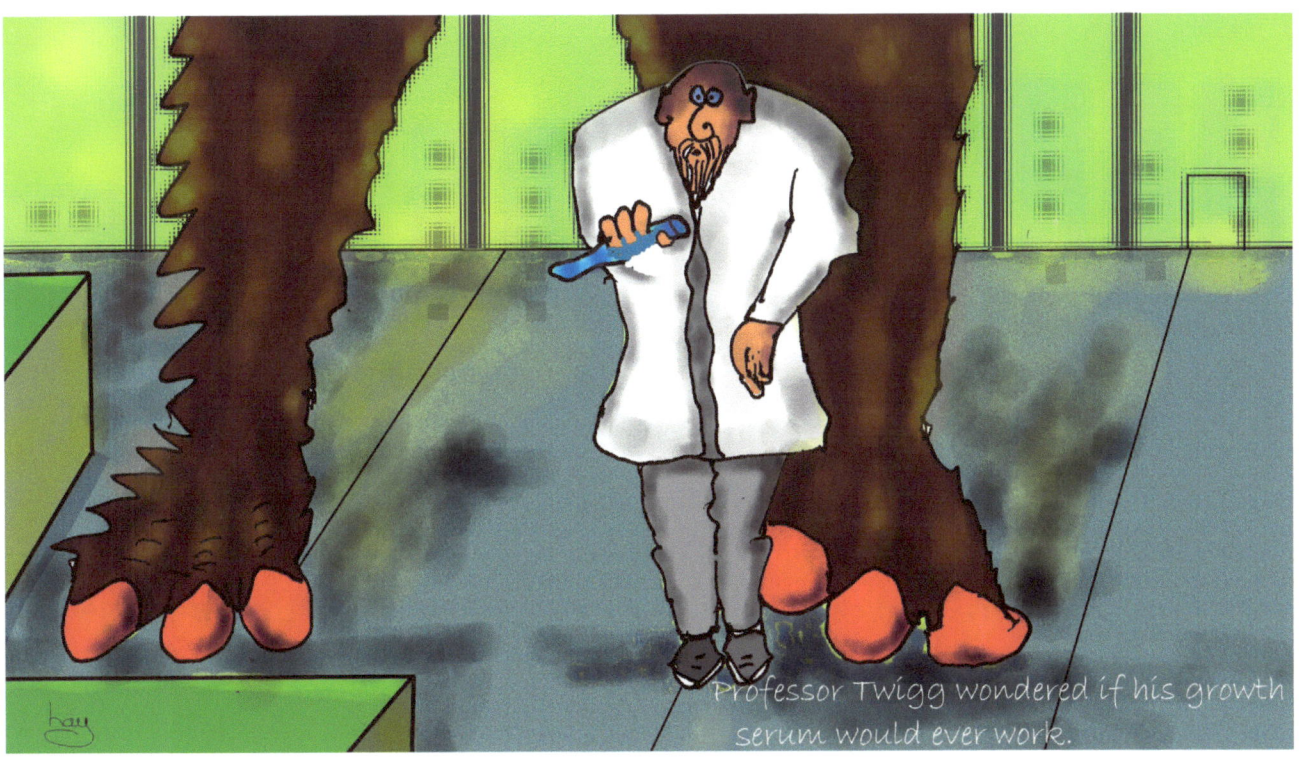

Professor Twigg wondered if his growth serum would ever work.

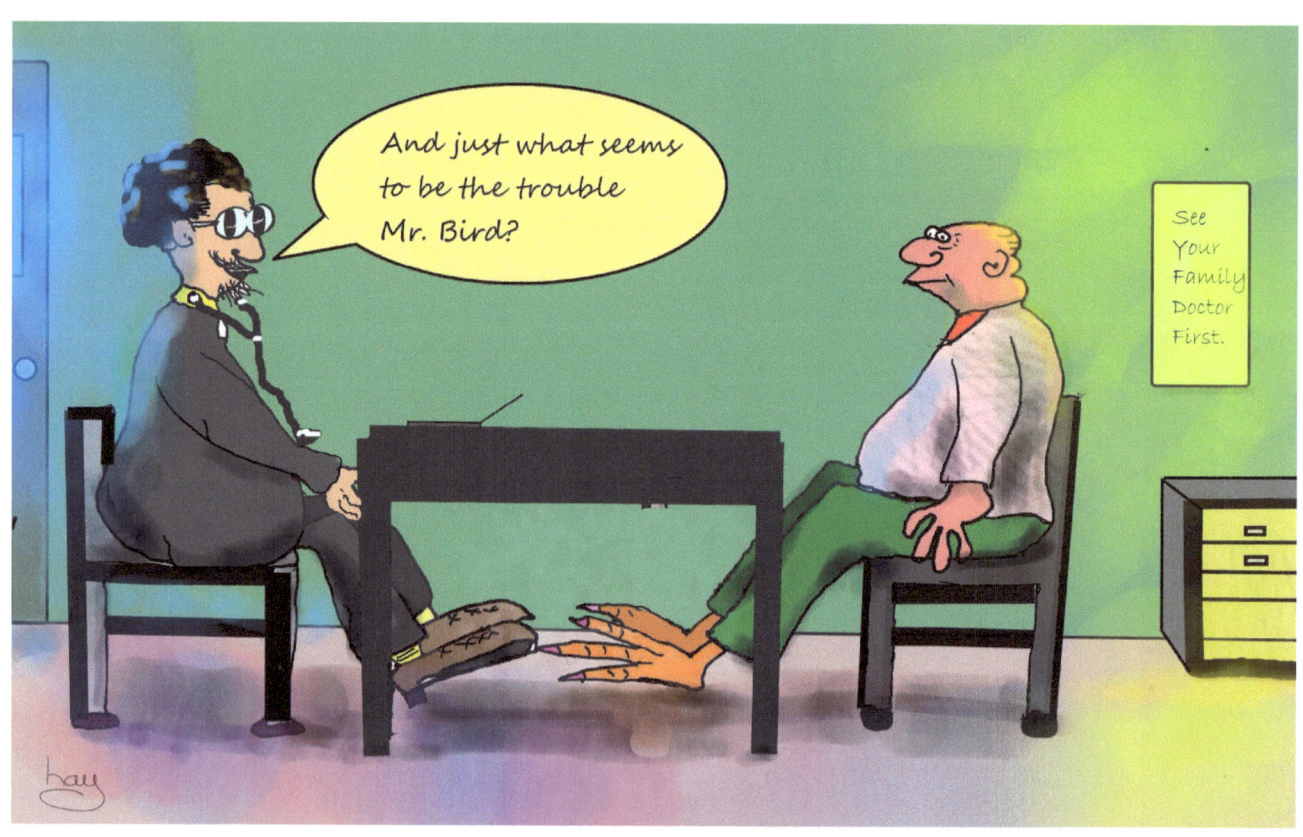

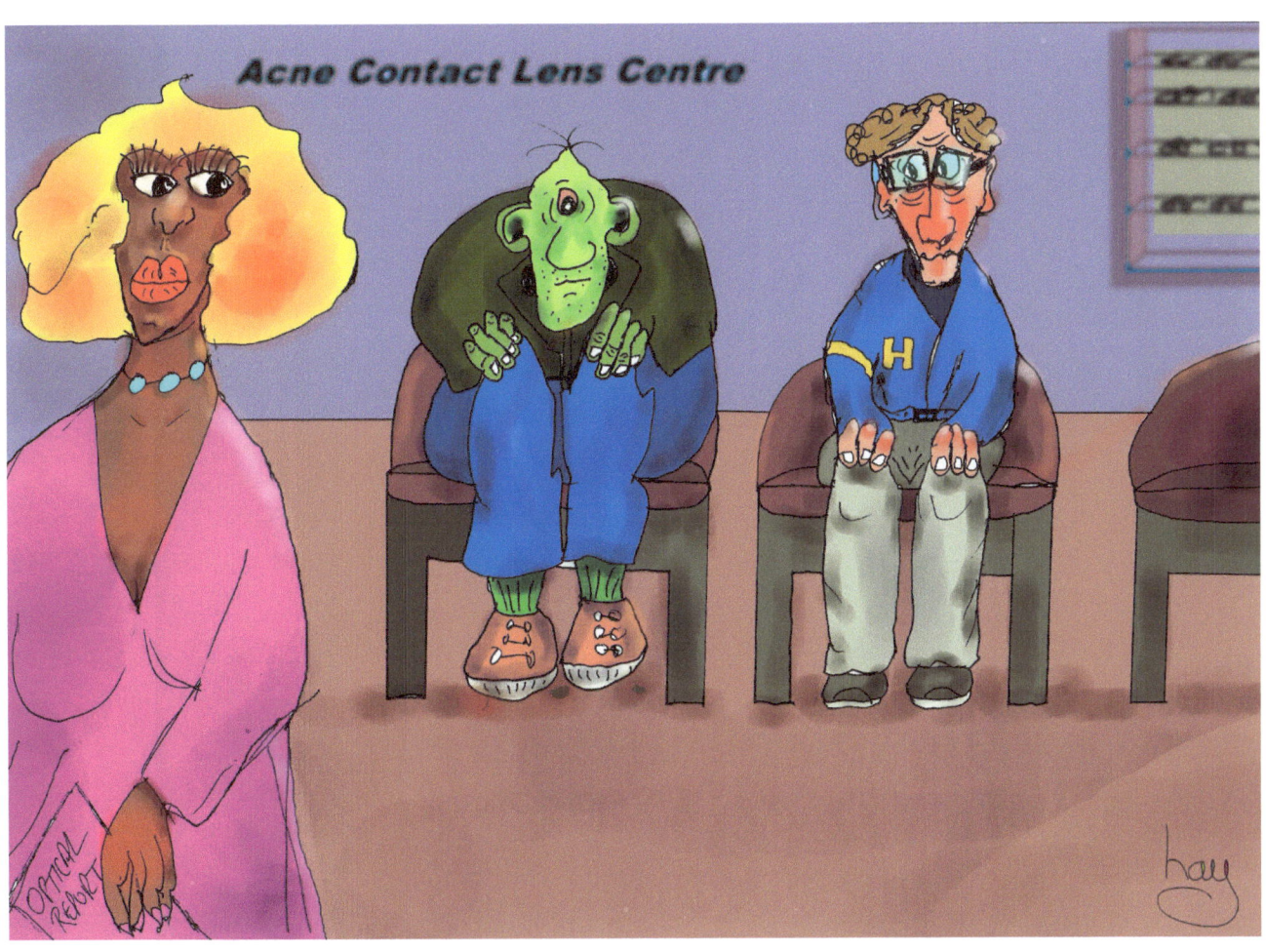

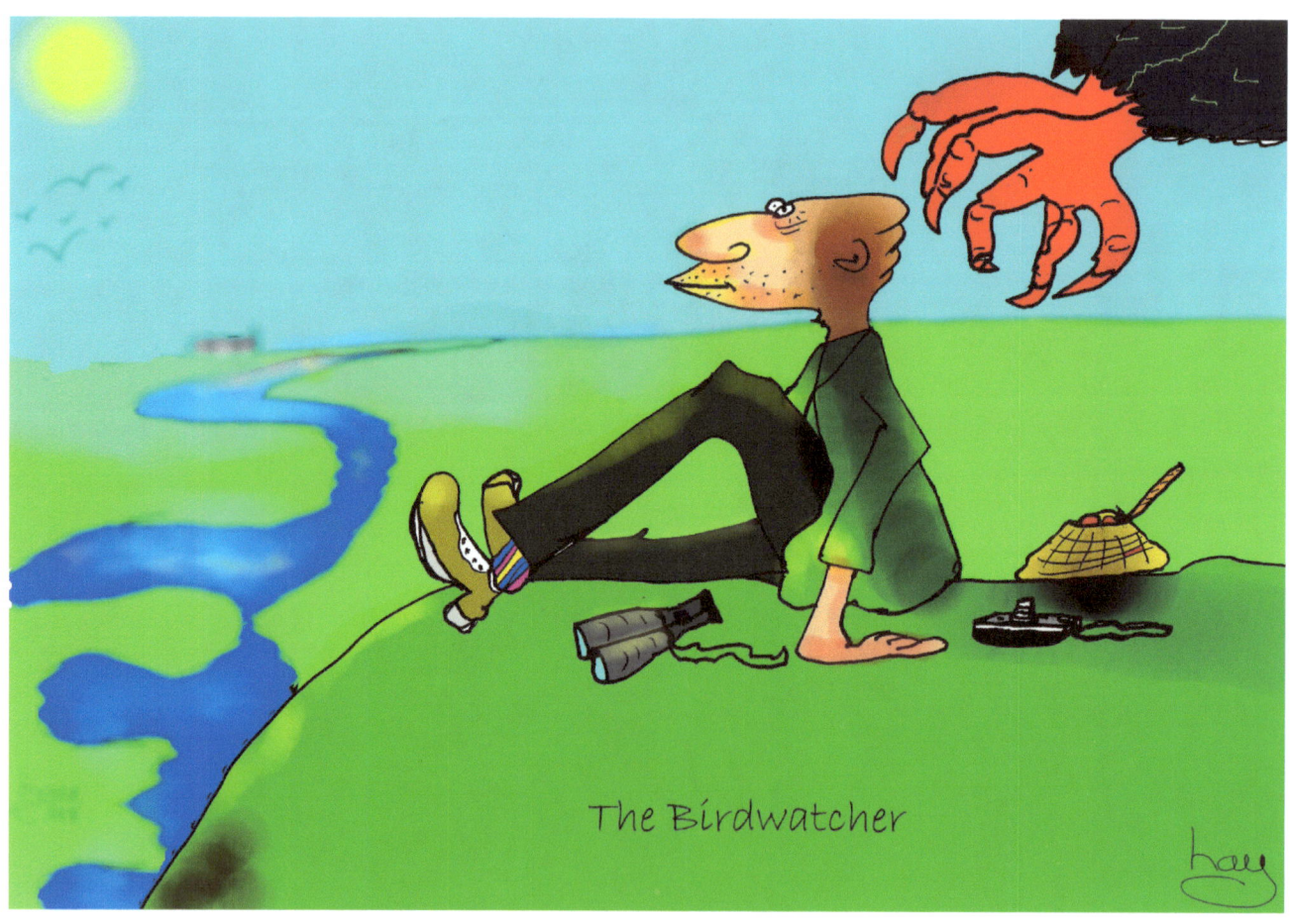

The Birdwatcher

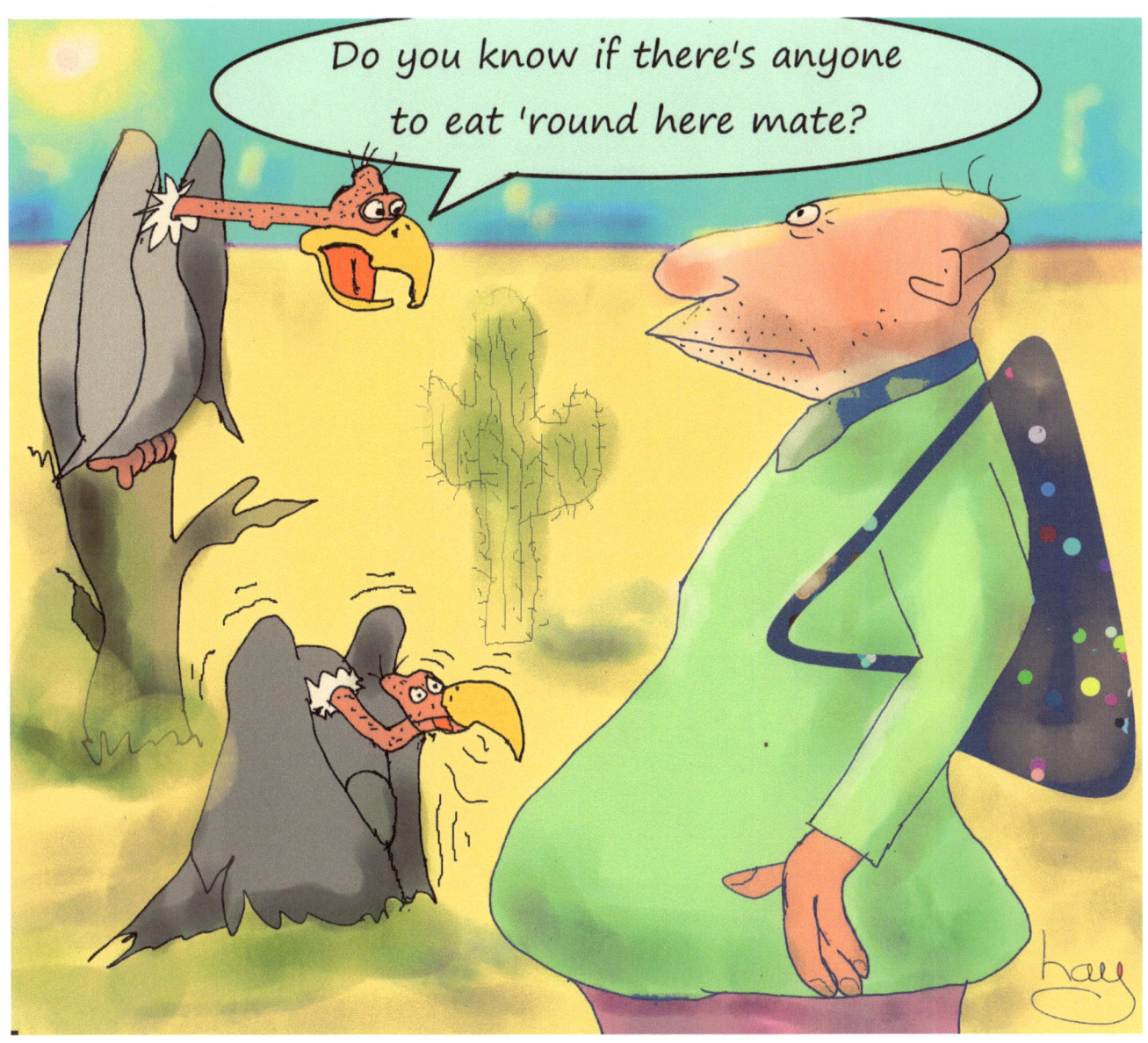

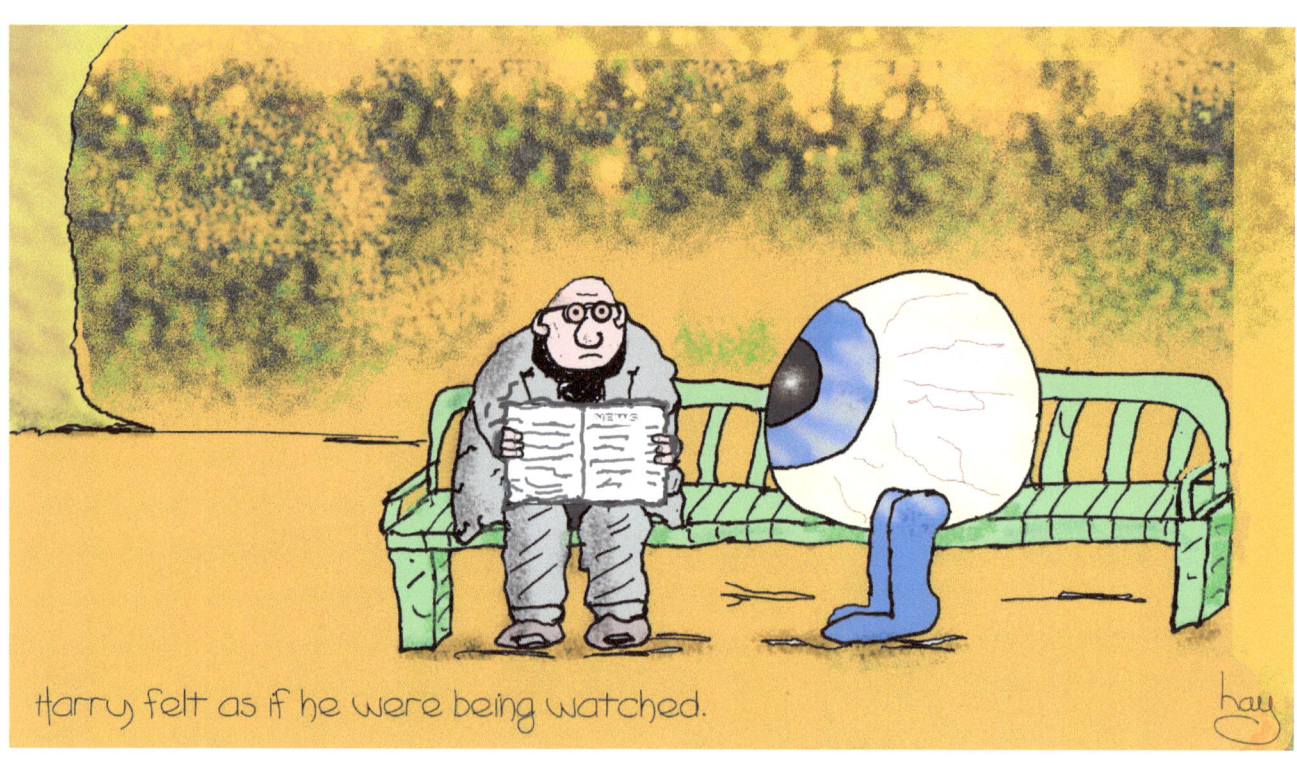

Harry felt as if he were being watched.

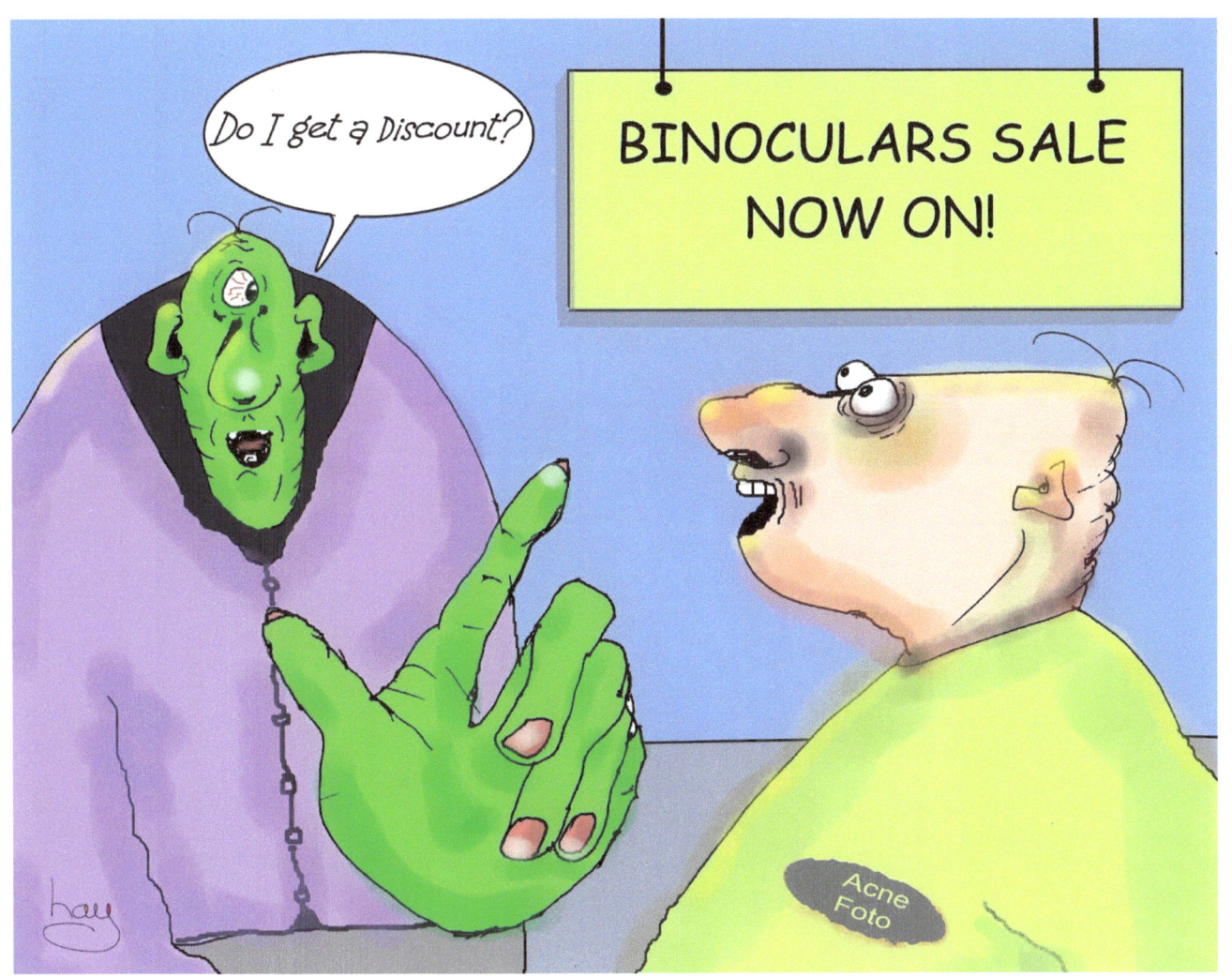

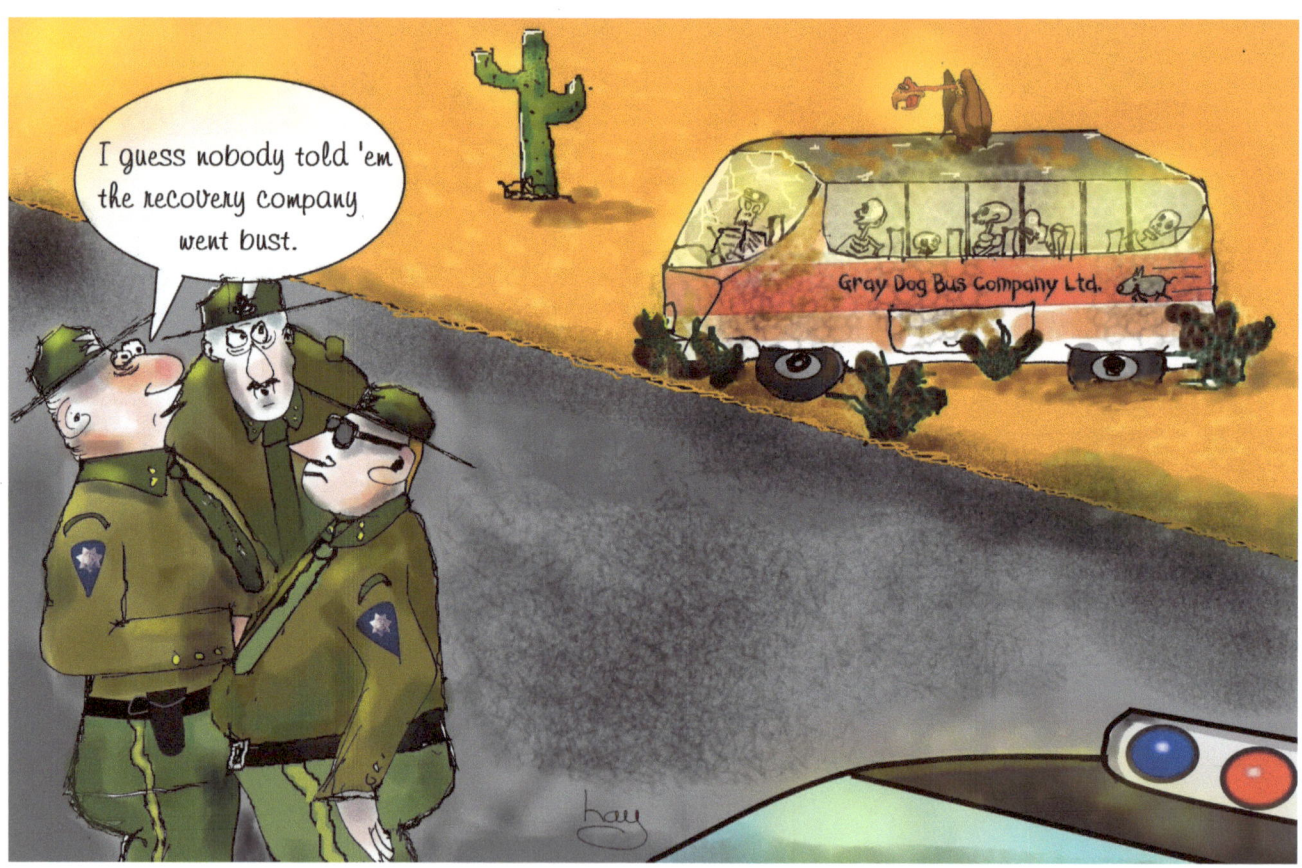

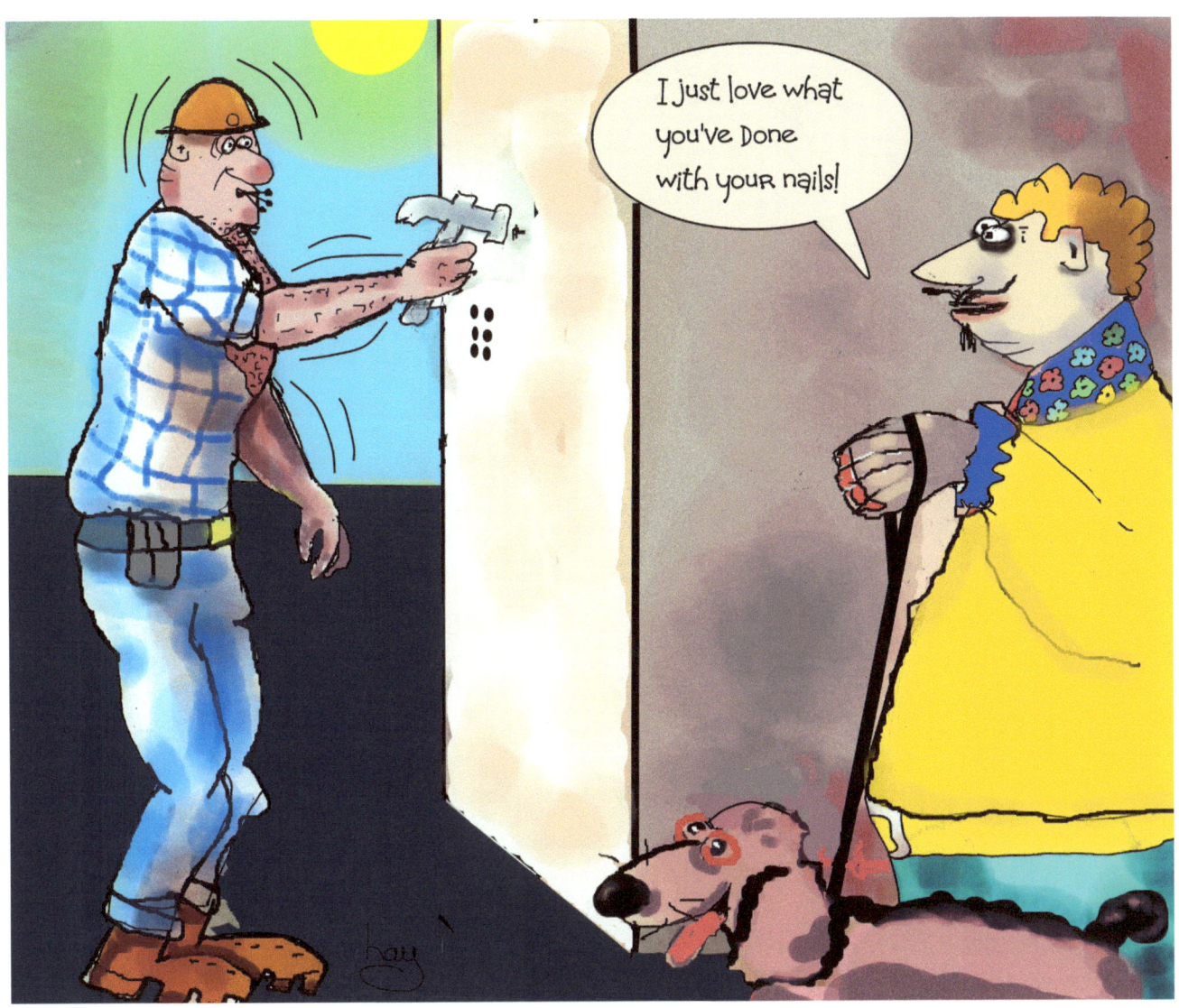

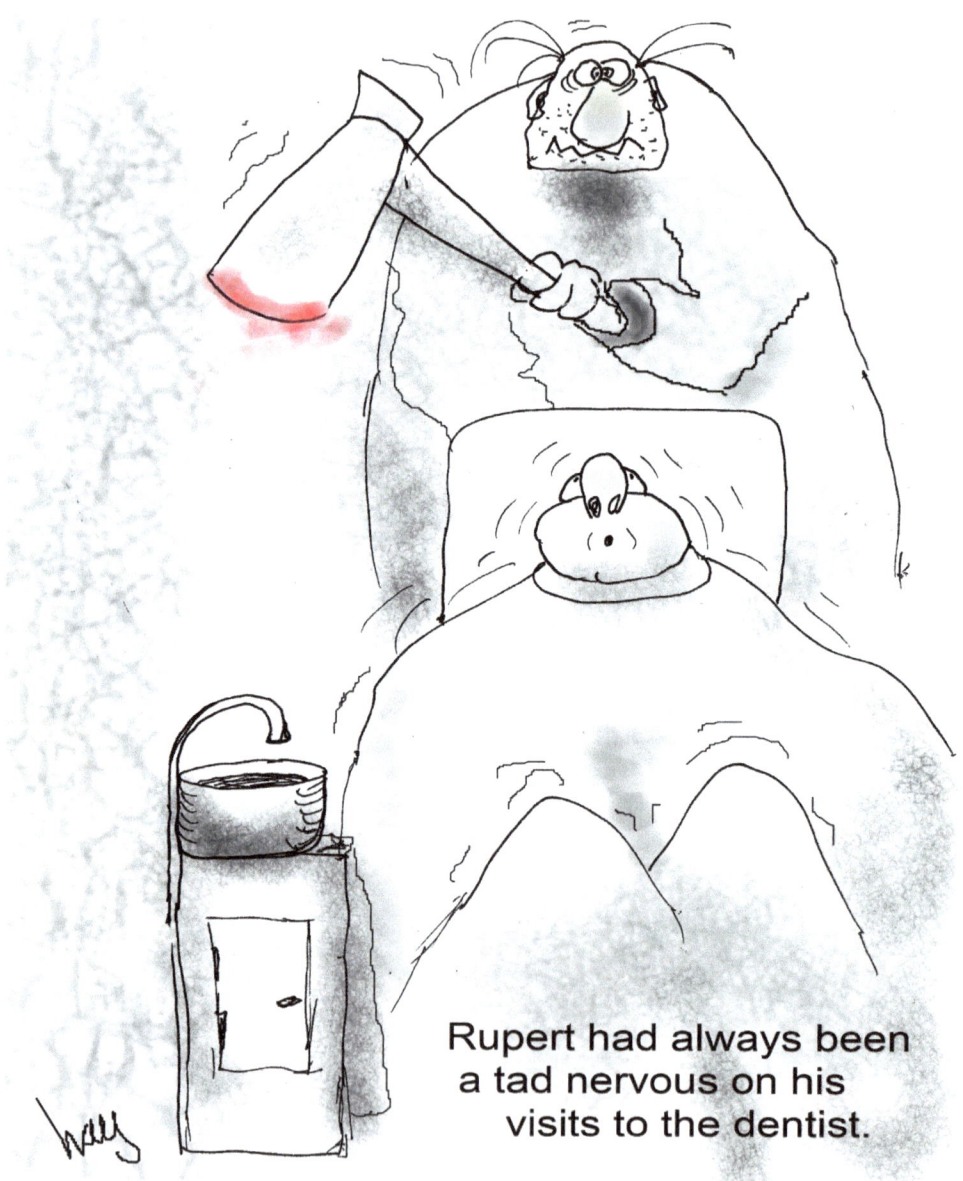

Rupert had always been
a tad nervous on his
visits to the dentist.

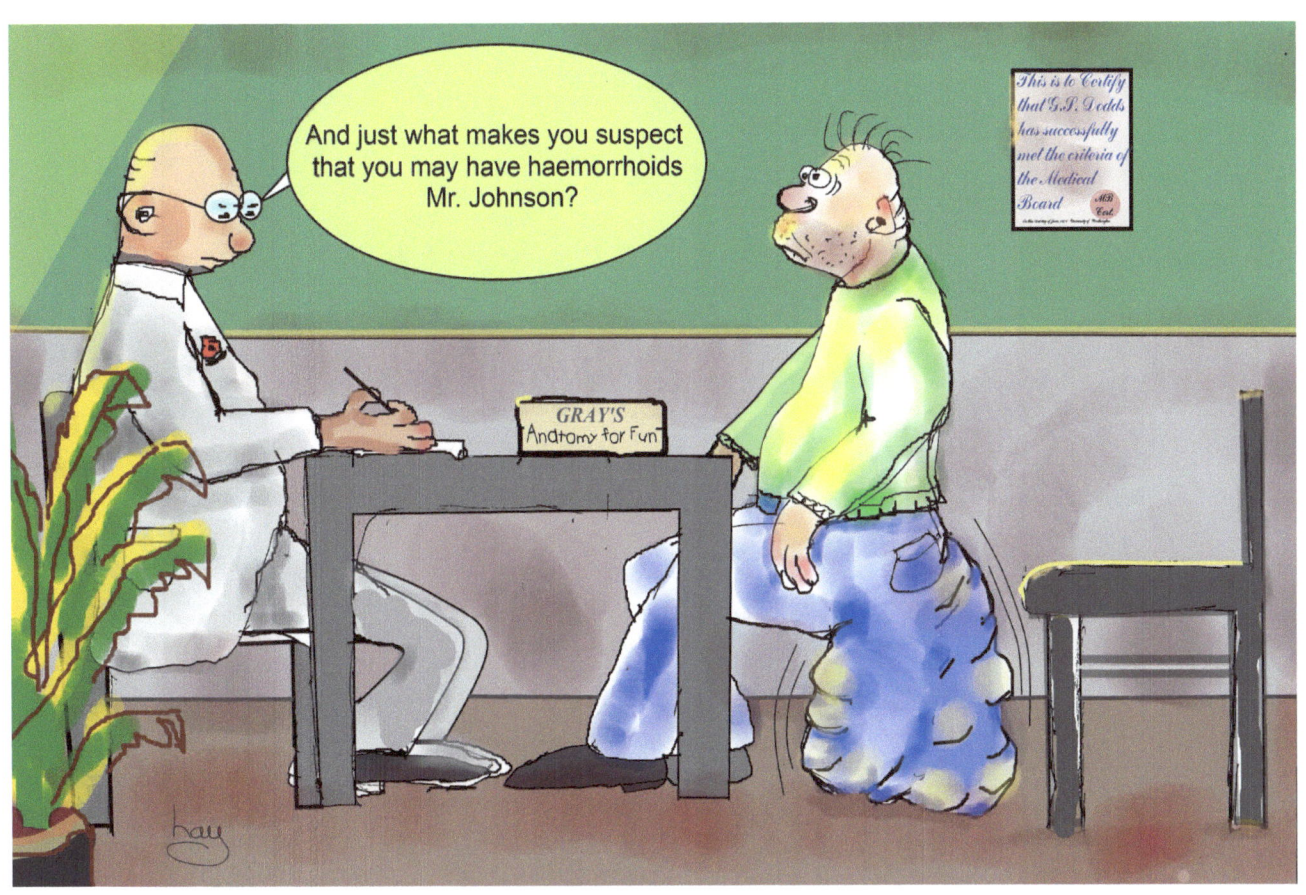

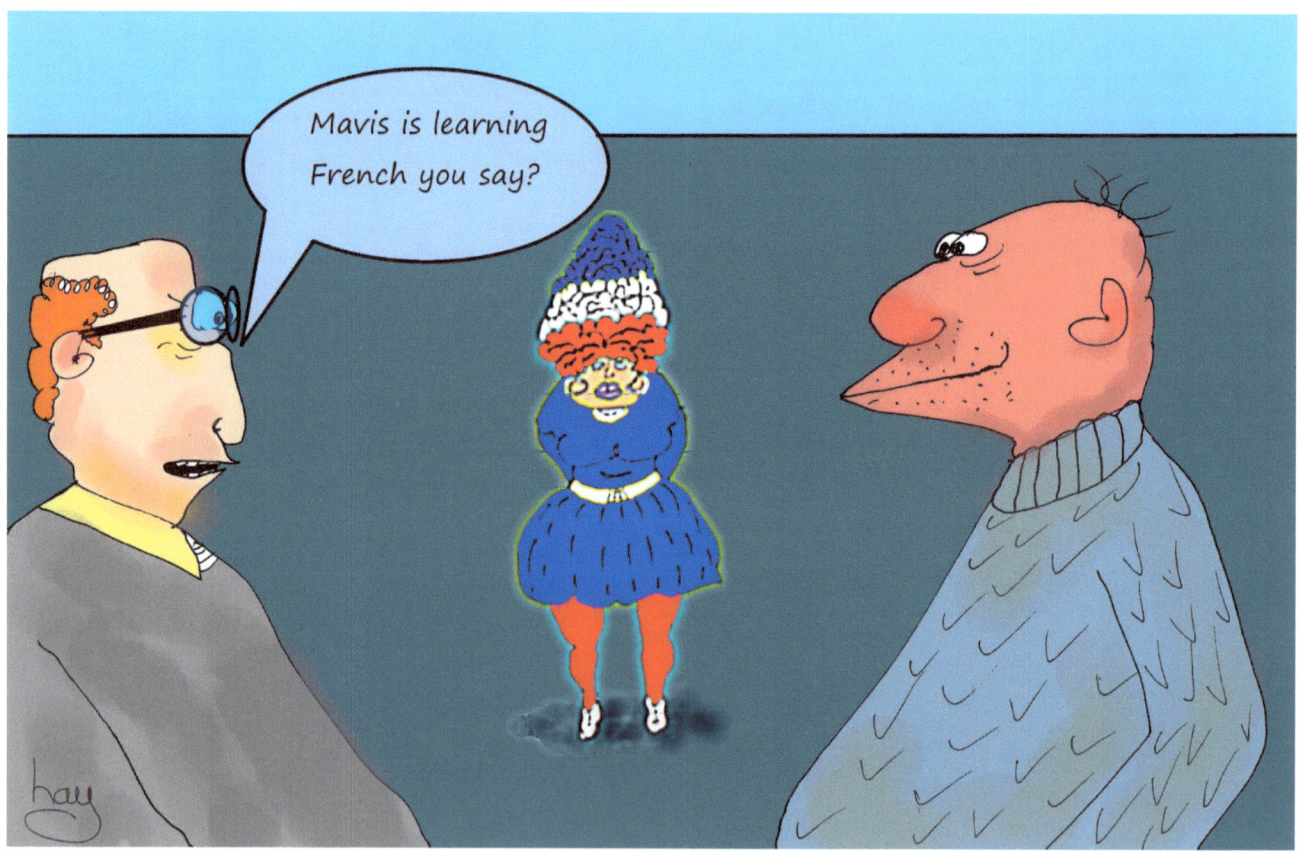

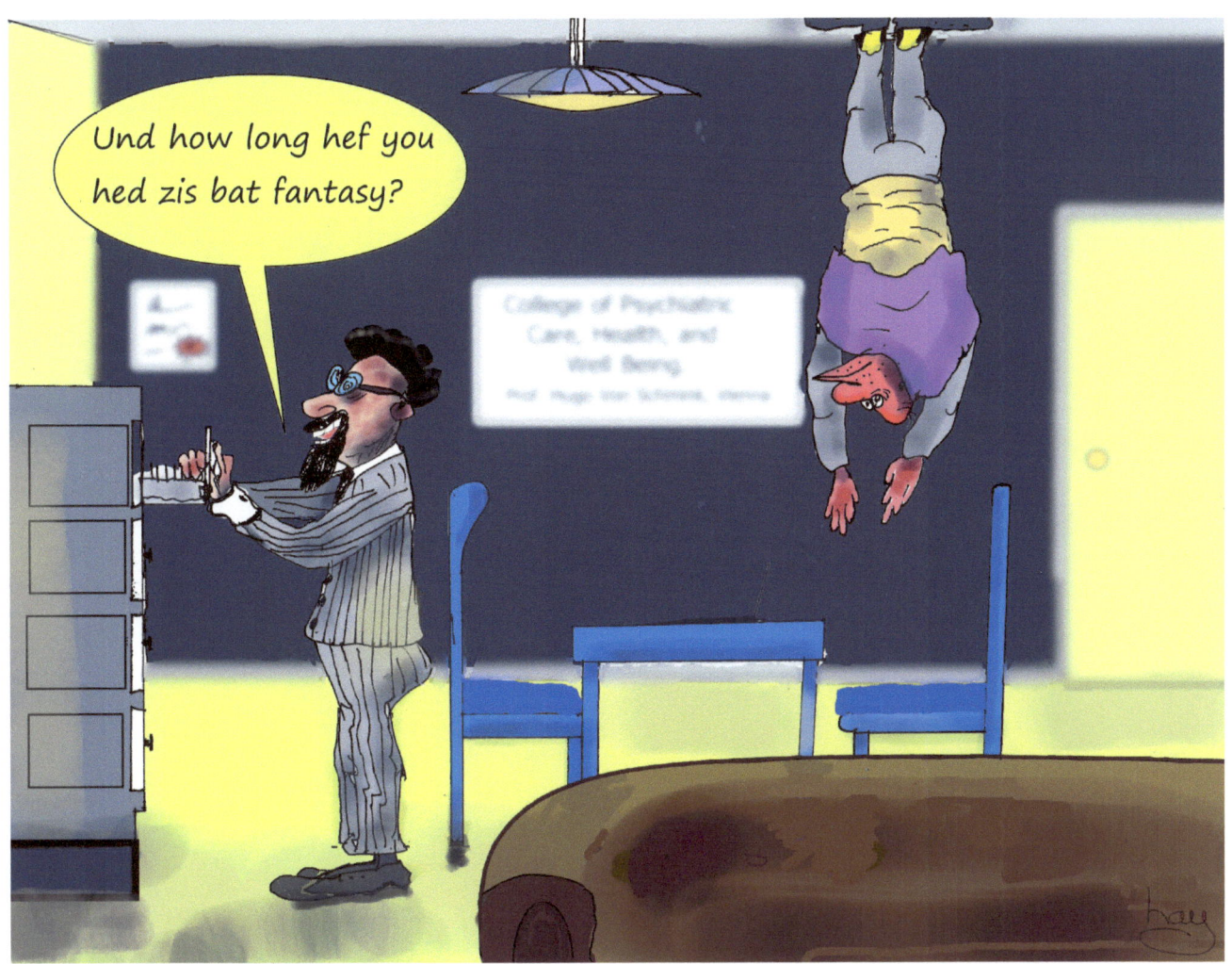

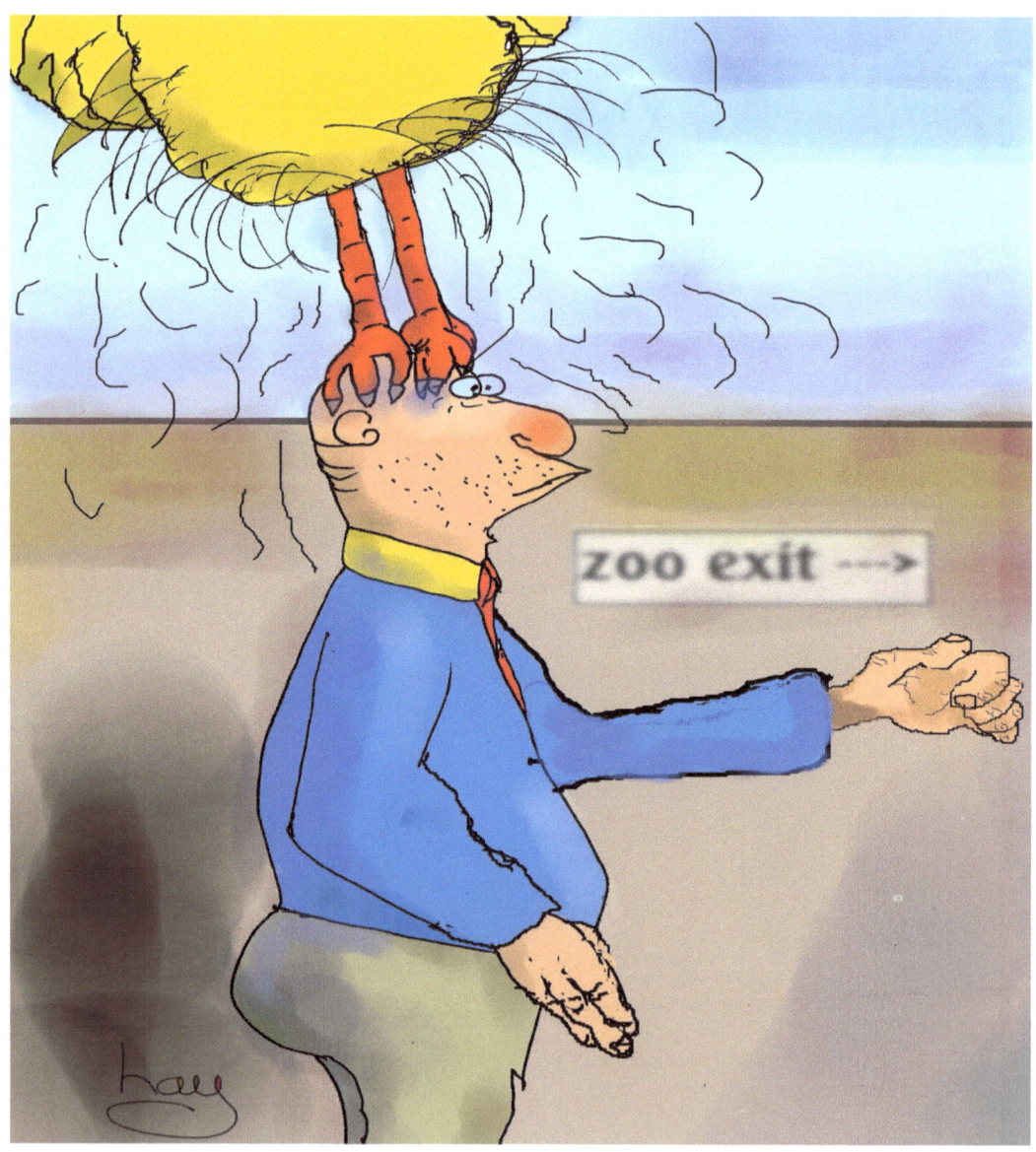

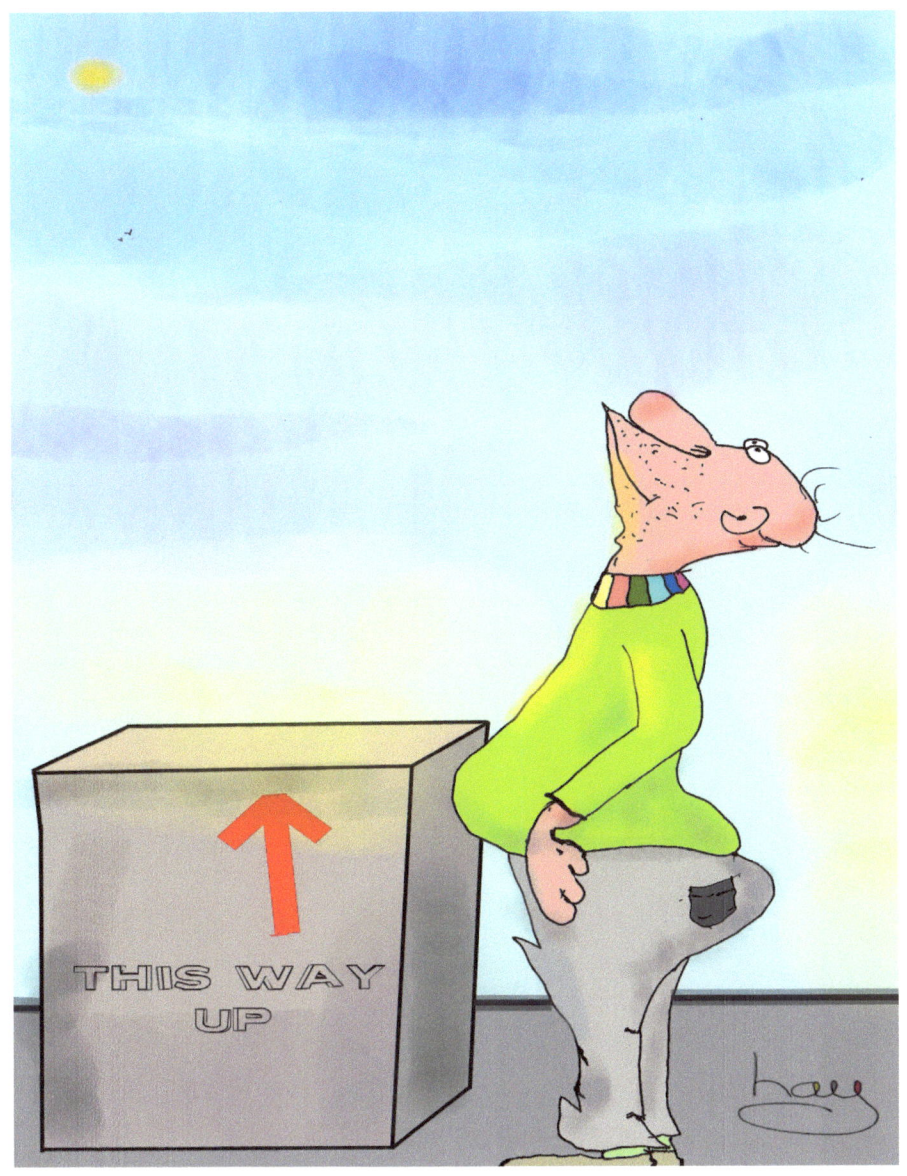

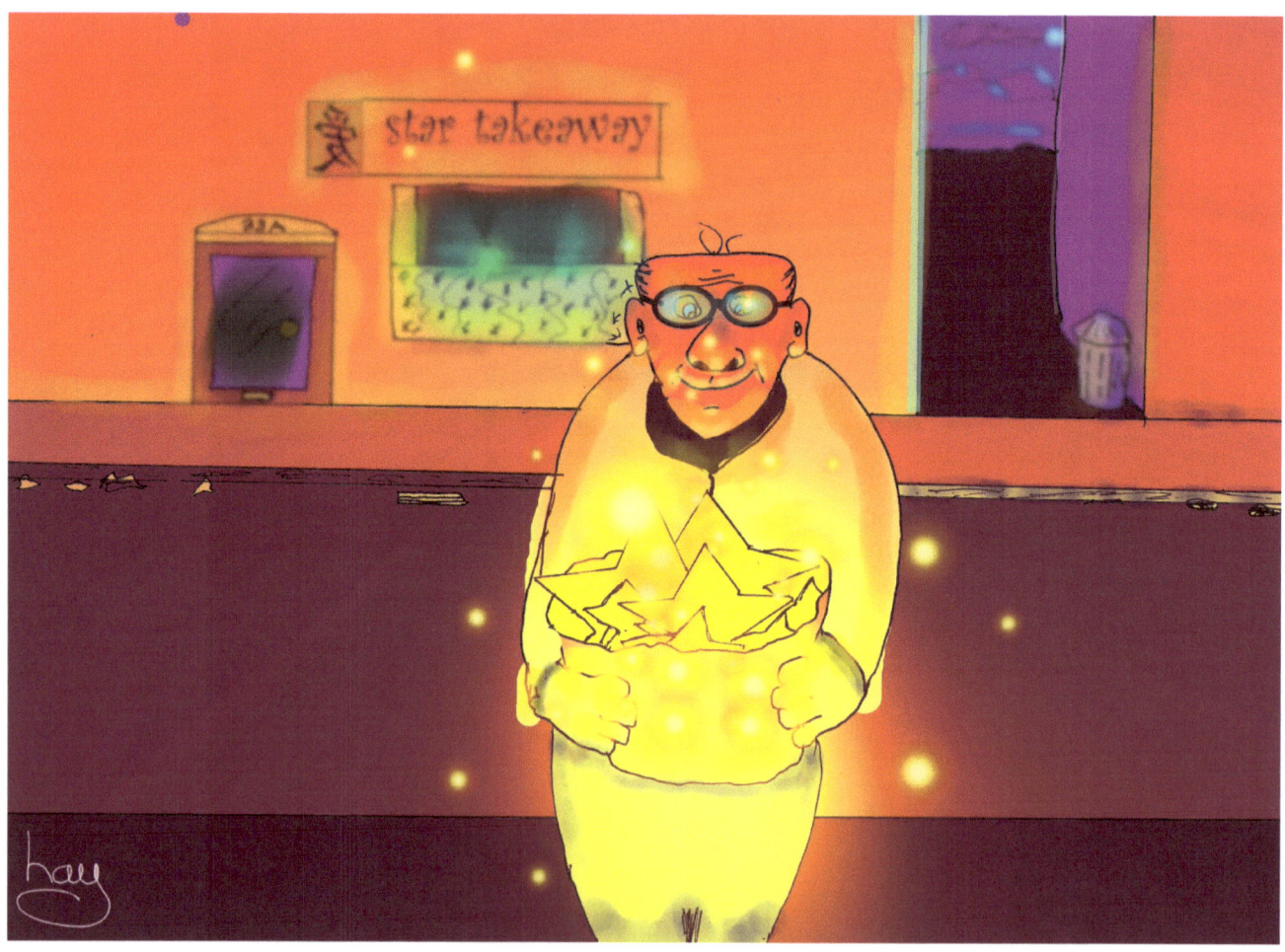

Other books by this author:

POETRY SCHMOETRY

A collection of fifteen poems that run the gamut from love, humour, tragedy, satire and all things in between.

If you love words and language as much as the author, then no doubt you'll enjoy his imagery, rhythm, and inventiveness. Sure to become a little treasure. (available as an e-book and in print)

FUCK OFF!

A tale of hope, love, despair, frustration, foul language and Tourette's.

This hilarious romp follows the adventures of a young Londoner with Tourette Syndrome. Full of weird and outrageously dressed characters, including sexy Italian starlets, masochistic yobs, media lovies and just plain folk, this romantic comedy will warm your heart and question your sanity. Have fun. (this novel is available as an e-book and in print)

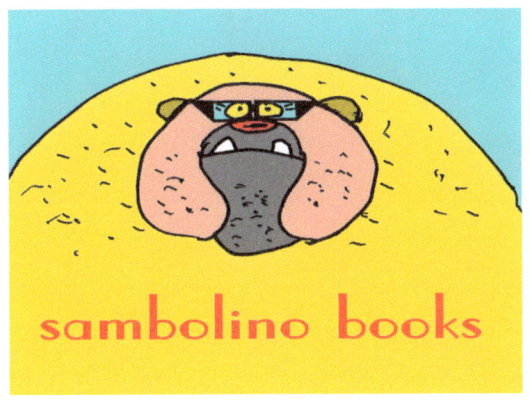

Sambolino Books Hertfordshire England